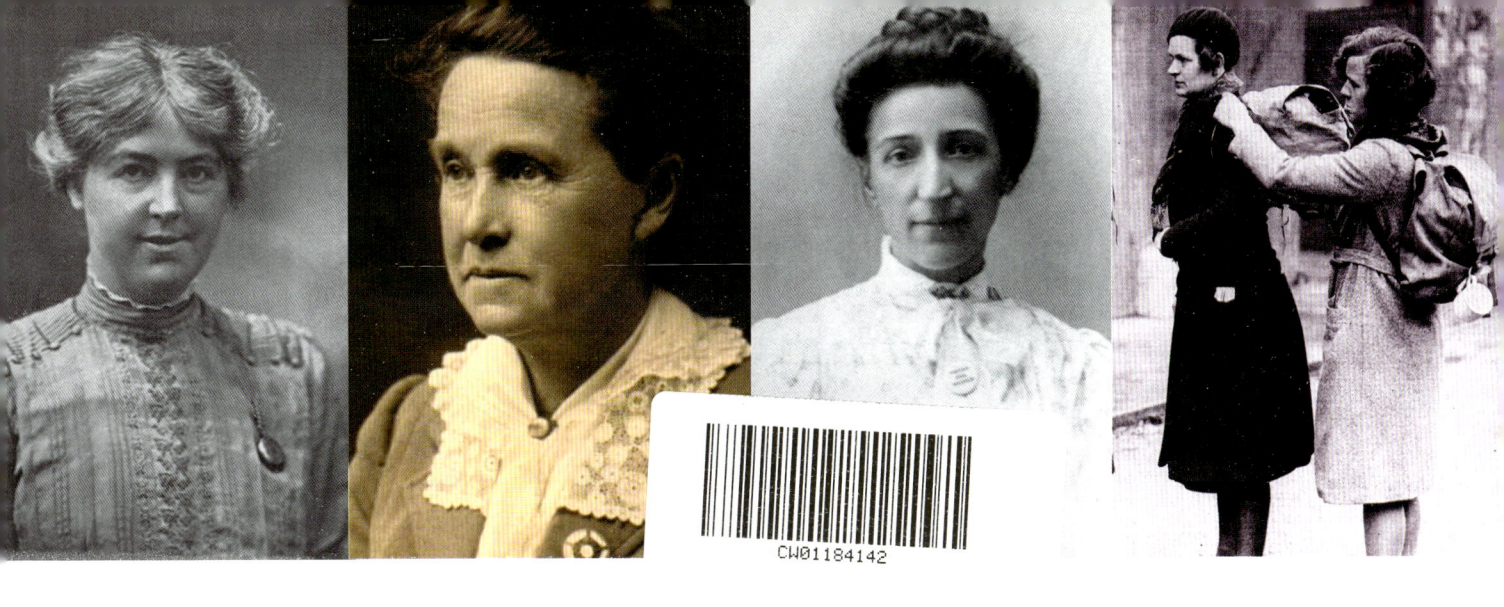

Contents

Introduction	2
Women and the First World War "You are to have a military mind and to think as you are told to think."	3
Women in the 1920s "Labour women have proved themselves the most magnificent fighters..."	15
Women in the 1930s "Work Work Work, We want work, And an end to the Means Test..."	29
Women and the Second World War "Get the women organised, and then we can end the war this year."	43
Afterword: Ellen Wilkinson's Peace 1945-1947	57
About the Mary Quaile Club	62
Previous Mary Quaile Club publications	65

Introduction

This publication is a sequel to my previous work, *"Up Then Brave Women"* (2012), which told the story of Manchester's radical women from the fields of Peterloo in 1819 up to the partial suffrage victory of 1918 when women aged over 30 gained the vote after an epic struggle stretching back some sixty years.

But this sucess took place against the immense slaughter of the First World War, leading the ever-perceptive Sylvia Pankhurst - one of the architects of the suffrage victory - to comment bitterly,"Saddened and oppressed by the great world tragedy, by the multiplying graves of men, and the broken hearts of women, we hold aloof from such rejoicings; they stride with a hollow and unreal sound upon our consciousness."

In *"For the sake of the women who are to come after"* I hope to rescue from obscurity women whose stories deserve to remembered – and celebrated. I believe that this history can and should inspire working people today who continue to face deep-rooted economic, social and political problems.

I begin with the First World War and its transformative effect (for a time at least) on the range and scope of women's employment as women were recruited by the tens of thousands to work in the war industries. Women trade unionists from the two Manchester Women's Trades Councils campaigned to ensure that women were paid properly and enjoyed good working conditions.

I also document the brave efforts of women activists (many of them former suffragists and suffragettes and a good few hailing from Manchester), who sought not to stop the war (for that would have been a foolish dream), but to start a discussion on how such an appalling event could be prevented from ever happening again.

Getting the vote proved to be a false dawn for women. Whilst the men in the main political parties - Labour and Conservative - were now happy to canvass women voters for their support, they were extremely reluctant to step aside and allow women into Parliament. The number of women MPs in the Commons remained but a handful for many years. One of the few was Ellen Wilkinson, a Manchester trade unionist and suffragist, who became the MP for Middlesbrough in 1924 and Jarrow in 1935. She played a very active role in the trade union and labour movement. Indeed, it is hard to find a progressive campaign or organisation between the wars that Ellen was not involved with in some way as I show in these pages.

Women made a limited incursion into local government with women such as Annie Lee, Hannah Mitchell and Ellen Wilkinson being elected onto Manchester City Council, where they attempted to advance the interests of women. Annie sought to ensure that women local government employees were not sacked on getting married, Hannah campaigned for practical improvements to women's lives such as washhouses, while Ellen raised the issue of unemployed women.

Industrial struggles in the 1920s culminated in the General Strike in May 1926. Whilst women workers were not called out on strike by the Trades Union Congress, women played a very active role in a forgotten solidarity movement, organised by Ellen Wilkinson and other women in the labour movement, to raise money to support mining families who continued on strike until the autumn after they had been abandoned by the TUC.

The Wall Street crash of October 1929 precipitated a worldwide recession which led to mass unemployment around the globe, including Britain, where the numbers out of work topped three million. The National Unemployed Workers' Movement fought for the rights of the unemployed, particularly after 1931 when the hated Means Test reduced families to penury. Women from Lancashire took part in four national hunger marches in 1930, 1932, 1934 and 1936.

Economic collapse produced political disorder. Fascist movements spread across Europe, culminating in the Nazi takeover of Germany in 1933. At home women such as Evelyn Taylor took on Oswald Mosley's British Union of Fascists, whilst abroad Molly Murphy and Lillian Urmston served as nurses on the Republican side during the Spanish Civil War.

War returned to Europe, and indeed the world, in September 1939. Women went out to work again in the war industries, while their husbands, brothers and sons went off to war. But many women also had to suffer an additional emotional trauma when more than 50,000 children from Manchester were evacuated out of the city on 1 September.

During the war there was intense discussion on what kind of world would come into being when the conflict finally ended. Women came together to debate these issues in the forgotten Women's Parliaments movement which held its Lancashire meeting in Manchester on 12 April 1942.

This historical survey ends in 1945, but, with Ellen Wilkinson having been referred to on numerous occasions in these pages, it seemed right and proper to add an Afterword which takes her story through her years as Minister of Education and up to her early and unexpected death in the depth of bitter winter in February 1947.

Women and the First World War

"You are to have a military mind and to think as you are told to think."

The First World War broke out in the summer of 1914 after the assassination in Sarajevo of Archduke Franz Ferdinand, heir to the Austro-Hungarian Empire, on 28 June unleashed a diplomatic crisis between the European Powers which ended in France and Russia going to war against Germany and Austria. Britain declared war on Germany on 4 August. By the time the conflict ended in November 1918 the number of dead and injured ran into millions, while the political map of Europe was changed forever as the Austro-Hungarian, Ottoman and Russian Empires disintegrated and a slew of new countries emerged in their wake. Nothing would ever be the same again.

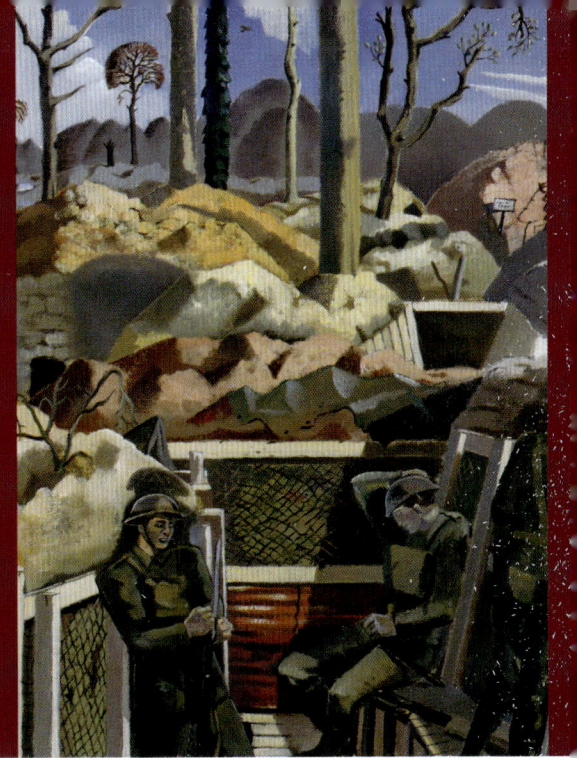

The Outbreak of War

In July 1914 the International Women's Suffrage Alliance (IWSA) was holding its annual meeting in London, where it was based. The Alliance was founded in 1904 to bring together suffrage campaigns in different countries. On 30 July, when they realised that war was imminent, they quickly drafted an International Manifesto of Women which was presented to the British Foreign Minister, Edward Grey, and to every European ambassador in London. Even as they delivered the letter, millions of armed men were on the move:

We, the women of the world, view with apprehension and dismay the present situation in Europe, which threatens to involve one continent, if not the whole world, in the disasters and horrors of war. In this terrible hour, when the fate of Europe depends on decisions which women have no power to shape, we, realising our responsibilities as the mothers of the race, cannot stand passively by. Powerless though we are politically, we call upon the governments and powers of our several countries to avert the threatened unparalleled disaster ... We women of twenty-six countries, having banded ourselves together in the International Women's Suffrage Alliance with the object of obtaining the political means of sharing with men the power which shapes the fate of nations, appeal to you to leave untried no method of conciliation or arbitration for arranging international differences which may help to avert deluging half the civilised world in blood.[1]

On 3 August the *Manchester Guardian* published a selection of letters from a number of well-known public figures arguing in favour of Britain remaining neutral, including one from Emily Hobhouse, an anti-war campaigner who had exposed the dreadful ill-treatment of Boer civilians in British concentration camps during the Boer War. She wrote from Oxford:

May I add my name to the many who are endorsing your demand for England's neutrality, and who are thanking you for the calmness and wisdom with which you advocate a policy of peace. Few English people have seen war in its nakedness. Hence their thoughtless cry for it. They know nothing of the poverty, destruction, disease, pain, misery, and mortality that follow in its train and fall chiefly upon innocent labouring people. I have seen all this and more, and my experience and knowledge of those awful things add force to my appeal to all lovers of humanity to rise up and avert the horror that is threatened.[2]

On the last day of peace the hastily formed Neutrality League, founded by Sir Norman Angell, held an evening meeting in Stevenson Square, Manchester, to advocate that Britain stay out of the war. Some two thousand people attended, and, despite attempts by a group of about 50 people to disrupt the meeting by singing the National Anthem and "Rule Britannia," the majority supported the resolution which protested "against the manner in which the government is forcing us into war." The sole woman speaker on the platform was the socialist and suffragette Annot Robinson, who spoke of the horrors of war and the effect on women and children in the home. At eleven o'clock that same evening the British government's ultimatum to Germany expired and war was declared.

The following day a crowded meeting was held in Milton Hall to protest at Britain going to war, presided over by Sir Alexander Porter, with many members of Manchester and Salford Councils present. Councillor Margaret Ashton, (a leading Manchester suffragist) was one of the speakers, the only woman on the platform. She said that she was there to voice the feeling of the women and children, "not only of Britain but of the world," and called on those present to protest "with their whole soul" and leave no stone unturned "to save the country from this desolation which is a crime against humanity." The meeting passed a resolution which stated that the government ought to have maintained neutrality and protested against "being dragged into war."

But the war was already unstoppable. The British Expeditionary Force sailed to

France: the first British soldier to die was Private John Parr, a bicycle scout, killed on 21 August, near Mons, the first of over 700,000 soldiers, sailors, airmen and civilians to lose their lives.

Robert Roberts, who lived in Salford where his mother ran a shop, recalled in his memoirs *The Classic Slum* how the declaration of war was received in his street:

The fourth of August 1914 caused no great burst of patriotic fervour among us. Little groups, men and women together (unusual, this) stood talking earnestly in the shop or at the street corner, stunned a little by the enormity of events. But soon public concern yielded to private self-interest. A rush of customers to the shop gave us the first alarm – sugar, flour, bread, butter, margarine, cheese, people began frantically to buy all the food they could find money for. 'Serve no strangers!' my mother ordered after the first hour. 'Only "regulars" from now on.' At once she dispatched us children in relays to join queues already formed outside Lipton's and Maypole Dairy and other multiple grocers on the high road. One day of our foraging, I remember, brought in 28 lbs of margarine and 20 lbs of sugar, which my mother promptly sold off in small lots at a penny a pound profit.[3]

The Labour Party came out in support of the war, clear evidence that, once the government had declared war, many people felt duty bound to support their country and its armed forces, setting aside their previous doubts and inclination towards neutrality.

With fighting already taking place in Belgium, as the German army besieged Liège, there was an immediate chilling effect on anti-war views. On 7 August, for instance, a meeting of the Manchester and Salford Trades Council took place at the Clarion Cafe on Market Street, Manchester, presided over by leading trade unionist (and future Labour MP) Alf Purcell. They decided not to proceed with the anti-war meeting which they had been planning to hold the following Sunday in the Free Trade Hall with Ramsay MacDonald one of the main speakers.

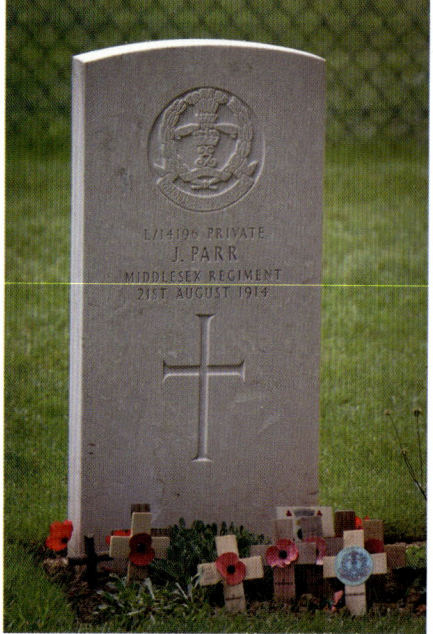

The grave of John Parr, the first British soldier to be killed

Instead they passed a resolution which said that the meeting strongly deplored:
the apparent failure to settle the international difference by conciliation or arbitration and view with horror the crime of the European war, which we consider is the result of secret understandings and alliances of which the mass of the working classes know nothing and on which they have never been consulted. We are of the opinion that the conflict will leave mankind the poorer, will set back civilisation and will be a powerful check to the amelioration of the condition of the working classes. Seeing that the democracy of the nations concerned have no quarrel with each other, we stand by the efforts of the international working class movement to bring the present trouble to a speedy end.[4]

The Quakers had arranged a meeting for 9 August to protest at the possibility of Britain being drawn into the war and, although overtaken by events, they still went ahead with this in their Meeting House on Mount Street, Manchester. The first speaker was the Quaker Lady Barlow, who told the packed hall that they were not assembled to criticise the government for, she said, there were "good, high-minded men in it" who had come to their present conclusion "after deep thought" and there were "noble men" who had left the Cabinet rather than be parties to the war policy. They of the Society of Friends had come together to state again their principle that "war was not in the spirit of Christ."

Margaret Ashton also spoke and said that the war pointed to the failure of "our so-called Christianity and civilisation" and that they had "no quarrel with any of the peoples of the earth." She posed a number of questions to the audience: "What have we been doing that the governments have been allowed to believe that might was right? Was it not clear that Christians had denied Christ in permitting this war?...Who would be the better when the war was over? Who would gain anything in prosperity, in righteousness in such a war?"[5]

The declaration of war split both the socialist and the women's suffrage movements. Robert Blatchford, editor of the socialist newspaper *The Clarion*, and Henry Hyndman, leader of the British Socialist Party, both fully supported the war, bitterly attacking their former comrades who opposed the conflict as "Pro-German." By contrast the Independent Labour Party came out against the war with hundreds of its members becoming conscientious objectors. Its newspaper the *Labour Leader* openly published anti-war views in its columns, leading to its offices on Blackfriars Street, Manchester, being raided by the police on a number of occasions.

Both Emmeline and Christabel Pankhurst, the leaders of the militant suffrage organisation - the Women's Social and Political Union (WSPU) - came out fervently in support of the war, shutting down the WSPU campaign as soon as war was declared and changing the name of their newspaper from *The Suffragette* to *Britannia*. The government responded by releasing all suffragette prisoners. Over the next four years Emmeline travelled the length and breadth of the country speaking in favour of the war and attacking her former comrades who opposed the war. She also visited the USA in 1916 to raise money and to urge Americans to join the Allies against Germany and Austria, and even went to Russia in the spring of 1917 with Jessie Kenney in a vain attempt to

Annot Robinson

Millicent Fawcett

Helena Swanwick

keep the Russians in the war after the February Revolution, becoming friendly with the Women's Battalion of Death, formed by Maria Bochkareva.

Mrs Fawcett, leader of the National Union of Women's Suffrage Societies (NUWSS), the largest and most influential of the non-militant suffrage societies, also opted to support the war once it had started. The NUWSS announced that it was suspending its political work and was prepared to use its entire organisation for the help of those "who will be the sufferers from the economic and industrial revolution caused by the war."

Aside from Mrs Fawcett many leading members of the NUWSS were opposed to the war and these convictions eventually led to a split within the organisation. But, for the time being, the divisions within the leadership were papered over as NUWSS members engaged in relief and other work to alleviate the distress that many families suffered in the first months of the war as their menfolk joined up, jobs were lost and the price of goods went up.

On 10 November the Manchester and District Federation of the NUWSS (which had forty affiliated societies in the Manchester area) held its annual meeting in the Association Hall in Manchester, presided over by Margaret Ashton. Margaret told the audience that all political work had now ceased, and that the suffragists had thrown themselves zealously into all the work that lay upon non-combatants, men and women alike. Women suffragists, she continued, stood in a peculiar position of responsibility towards the nation because they claimed "both the privileges and duties of citizenship" and the duties of the non-combatant were quite as important and, in a way, as heavy as those of the men fighting at the front. The suffrage societies, Margaret concluded, had made use of this opportunity "in a remarkable manner."

The Secretary Mrs Tomlinson reported that the Federation's Manchester office had become the registration office for women voluntary workers wishing to undertake relief work. They had organised eight centres in co-operation with the Relief Committee for the feeding of nursing and expectant mothers and young children. They had also established two workrooms, employing 200 women, and also 30 skilled needlewomen who were making dolls. This work was controlled by the Women's Employment Sub-committee, chaired by Margaret Ashton, while Annot Robinson was the chair of the Relief Committee in Ancoats.

The elephant in the room was the fact that many suffragists in Manchester remained opposed to the war, and that the emphasis on relief work was sidestepping the issue. Finally, Mrs Eckhardt broke the silence on this topic by raising the possibility of an effort by organised women in the cause of peace. Margaret Ashton responded to her by deprecating discussion of the subject, asserting that there was a feeling that any discussion by the National Council of the NUWSS was inadvisable at the moment. Instead the matter would be considered in private by the Provincial Council of the NUWSS and the National Union might be able afterwards to make a statement. The meeting agreed to let the matter drop.

After the business meeting there was a public meeting at which the speakers included Helena Swanwick, a leading member of NUWSS in Manchester, who was also on the organisation's National Committee. She spoke about what form a peace settlement might take, and when she said that, speaking for herself as a suffragist, there was for her "no woman enemy in the world," she was cheered by the audience. Helena continued:

It was true that the women of all the nations wanted their own men to win; but they did not want only that – they wanted peace, and they would sacrifice something for peace. If we entered into this war to maintain democratic institutions and Parliamentary government, the sanctity of treaties and the rights of small nations, let them see to it that the settlement after the war embodies those principles...We go into a war saying one thing, and in the course of a few weeks we say another thing, and don't know that it is different

from the first. This grows upon us; it is a most invidious form of wickedness. We find it is possible for a man who calls himself a minister of God to say that it is no part of our duty to try to understand the mind of our enemies. He has gone a long way from the Christian religion, which teaches us to forgive our enemies, has he not? He says that what we have to do is not to think, because the starting of questions can only divide attention and damp enthusiasm. That is to say, we are not to think and not to try to understand in order that we may unquestioningly obey martial law...

It is being considered every week more wicked to think and to have a civilian mind. You are to have a military mind and to think as you are told to think. That seems to me a most terrible result of war.[6]

Women Workers

In the first months of the war there was a sharp rise in women's unemployment with clothing machinists, for instance, losing their jobs as manufacturers cancelled their autumn ranges. Those trade unions which organised women workers encouraged their unemployed members to apply to the Manchester Corporation Distress Committee, which had opened a workroom in the Heyrod Street Mission employing over a hundred women to make clothes.

However, as hundreds of thousands of men volunteered for the armed forces, shops and offices were forced to take on women to replace them, while the growing demands of the services generated more jobs in textiles, tailoring and allied trades, traditional areas of work for women. In 1915 women also began taking on traditional male jobs, working on the buses and trams as conductors, for instance, as the men in these occupations joined up.

By the summer of 1915 some 75,000 men had already been killed, whilst there was a severe shortage of munitions. The government now actively intervened to solve the problems in industry by passing the Munitions Act to facilitate the recruitment of women. This introduced what was known as "dilution" i.e. re-classifying traditional male skilled jobs in engineering as semi-skilled work that women would now be allowed to perform after an agreement with the relevant trade unions. The unions reluctantly accepted the introduction of women after the government promised that they would be sacked when the war ended.

At least a million women worked in munitions during the war, while hundreds of thousands of other women went into such trades as bleaching and dying and printing. They were even allowed to become mule spinners in Oldham, Bury and Rochdale, something previously bitterly resisted by the men in the Spinners' Union. This movement of women into work was accelerated after the introduction of conscription for men in 1916. By 1918 the number of women working in industry had risen from 3,276,000 to 4,808,000, many of whom had left domestic service to go into the factories.

The introduction of women into factories sometimes came as a shock to male pride. Salfordian Robert Roberts, whose father was an engineering worker, recalled in his memoirs:

My father was typical. In his cups he was wont to boast that, at the lathe, he had to manipulate a micrometer and work to limits of one thousandth of an inch. We were much impressed, until one evening in 1917 a teenage sister running a capstan in the iron works remarked indifferently that she too used a 'mike' to even finer limits. There was, she said, 'nothing to it'. The old man fell silent. Thus did status crumble! Before the end of the war more than 642,000 women had gone into government factories and engineering works of some sort, with millions more, men and women, doing manual work of almost every kind and developing new skills and new self-confidence on the way. The awe that many simpler souls had felt before the mystery of craft began to evaporate, to be replaced by at least some rational understanding.[7]

Roberts observed that the war gave women a greater self-confidence:

Wives in the shop no longer talked about 'my boss' or 'my master'. Master had gone to war and Missis ruled the household, or he worked close to her in a factory, turning out shell cases on a lathe and earning little more than she did herself. Housewives left their homes and immediate neighbourhood more frequently, and with money in their purses went foraging for goods even into the city shops, each trip being an exercise in self-education. She discovered her own rights... In the end the consequences of war, not the legal acquisition of female rights, released her from bondage.[8]

The Manchester, Salford and District Women's War Interests Committee

This Committee was set up in May 1915 to campaign for the rights of women workers to proper pay and conditions. The President was Margaret Ashton, the Joint Secretaries were Annot Robinson and Ellen Wilkinson. The Committee attempted to influence public opinion by carrying out investigations; by holding three well-attended conferences between 1915 and 1917; by holding public meetings; and by making representations to the Ministry of Munitions and local advisory committees.

In May 1915 the Committee began an investigation into the substitution of

Recruiting poster for women munition workers

Mary Qualle

Tea-break at British Oil Cake Company, Manchester

Margaret Ashton

women workers in traditionally male industries whose results they published the following year. The report noted that, since recruiting for the armed forces had been very successful in the Manchester area, the demand for women's labour had assumed a greater importance. Many previously male-only industries such as the trams, leather trades, railways and shops were now employing women for the very first time, while other occupations were opening branches and departments to women which had previously been closed to them. The Committee observed in the introduction:

Many labour and social problems have been or are being created by the entrance of large numbers of women, often entirely unorganised, into work which is a severe test of their health and physical endurance and which entails a revolution in their habits of life. Perhaps the problem set up by women doing men's work for women's traditional wages is one of the greatest at the moment, but there are others of the gravest importance also. The attitude of the men's Trade Unions, the utter absence of organisation amongst many of the women and the failure of attempts to organise them and the unsatisfactory position of women in controlled establishments are discussed, as well as the necessity for canteens and the effect of long hours and nightwork on the health of the women.[9]

The Manchester and Salford Women's Trades Union Council

Mary Quaile was the Organising Secretary for the MSWTUC throughout the First World War and worked very hard with other trade unionists to ensure that women workers were being paid properly. Many employers spouted patriotic slogans, but were very happy to use the replacement of male workers by women as an excuse to pay less and make more profit. The 1914 MSWTUC Annual Report asserted, "Never before has the organisation of women been so necessary as at present, as owing to the shortage of men through enlistment, women are being employed in their place and it is of the utmost importance that women doing the same work as men should receive the same wages."

In 1915 Mary did a great deal of organising work in the clothing trades, which had become very busy due to government contracts for the supply of uniforms. There were many disputes over prices and Mary accompanied the secretary of the Clothiers' Union on deputations to a number of firms, and on every single occasion they succeeded in obtaining higher wages. On occasions women workers took strike action: a strike at a blouse factory, for instance, ended after three days when the employer offered a higher wage.

Mary also helped set up a new union for women working in the tin box and canister Industry - the Association of Tin Box Makers - after canvassing nearly all the tin box workshops in Manchester. She acted as Secretary for the new union, which agitated for minimum rates at least equivalent to those set by the Trade Board for the industry. In July 1915 the government set up tribunals to resolve disputes between munition workers and employers, particularly on issues such as labour mobility, and Mary was appointed as an Assessor on a panel for the local Munitions Tribunal.

The 1915 MSWTUC Annual Report appealed for funds to carry on with the work of the MWTUC. "Never have funds for women's industrial organization been more needed than at the present time when the field of work has been indefinitely enlarged. It is clearly of the utmost importance alike to working men and women that the women replacing men in one industry after another should not bring down the old rates of pay, and it is equally clear that only prompt organisation can hinder this disaster."

In the early summer of 1916 Mary was able to establish a new union amongst women woodworkers employed in the making of munition cases following a dispute in a Newton Heath factory where the women were not being paid the rate for the job. Interestingly, three men's unions had approached the Women's War Interest Committee and the MSWTUC to ask them to organise the women, fearful perhaps that the introduction of women into the factory might undermine their pay.

In the autumn Mary and her assistant Kate Wallwork ran a campaign over the rates of pay for women working in the clothing trade where they had discovered that the experienced women were barely getting the Trade Board minimum. They met with a number of employers and succeeded in obtaining substantial wage increases in every case.

In June 1917 Mary gave evidence in person before a Commission on Industrial Unrest, headed by Judge Parr. She said that better allowances should be made to women who had men fighting abroad and that another point of discontent was "the quality and quantity of food."

After the end of the war the MSWTUC merged with Manchester Trades Union Council, with Mary becoming the Secretary of the Council's Women's Group, a position she held for many years.

Women Peace Campaigners

For the first six months of the war women opposed to the conflict struggled to make their voices heard amidst the patriotic clamour orchestrated by the government and the press. In January 1915, however, the IWSA newspaper *Jus Suffragi* carried an "Open Christmas Letter,"organised by Emily Hobhouse and signed by a hundred British women, which was addressed to "The Women of Germany and Austria." In the letter they declared that peace needed to be made in order to "to save the womanhood and childhood as well as the manhood of Europe." A number of women from Manchester were amongst the signatories, including Margaret Ashton and Annot Robinson.

Sisters, Some of us wish to send you a word at this sad Christmastide though we can but speak through the press. The Christmas message sounds like mockery to a world at war, but those of us who wished and still wish for peace may surely offer a solemn greeting to such of you who feel as we do. Do not let us forget that our very anguish unites us, that we are passing together through the same experience of pain and grief.

Caught in the grip of terrible circumstance, what can we do? Tossed on this turbulent sea of human conflict, we can but moor ourselves to those calm shores whereon stand, like rocks, the eternal verities - Love, Peace, Brotherhood.

We pray you to believe that come what may we hold to our faith in Peace and Goodwill between nations; while technically at emnity in obedience to our rulers, we owe allegiance to that higher law which bids us live at peace with all men.

Though our sons are sent to slay each other, and our hearts are torn by the cruelty of this fate, yet through pain supreme we will be true to our common womanhood. We will let no bitterness enter into this tragedy, made sacred by the life-blood of our best, nor mar with hate the heroism of their sacrifice. Though much has been done on all sides you will, as deeply as ourselves, deplore, shall we steadily refuse to give credence to those false tales so freely told us, each of the other?

In reply 155 German women sent sisterly greetings in a letter which was also published in *Jus Suffragi*:

To our English sisters, sisters of the same race, we express in the name of many German women our warm and heartfelt thanks for their Christmas greetings, which we only heard of lately.

This message was a confirmation of what we foresaw—that women of the belligerent countries, with all faithfulness, devotion, and love to their country, can go beyond it and maintain true solidarity with the women of other belligerent nations, and that really civilised women never lose their humanity...

The IWSA agreed to hold a Women's Congress at The Hague in neutral Holland in April 1915 to discuss the war and what kind of peace might be fostered when it finally ended. This initiative was fiercely opposed by Mrs Fawcett of the NUWSS, who denounced talk of peace at this time as akin to treason. After months of skirting around the issue, this issue led to a split within the NUWSS in March 1915 when 11 leading figures resigned their positions on the Executive, including Kate Courtney, Catherine Marshall and Helena Swanwick. Courtney wrote:

I have for some months felt strongly that the most vital work at this moment is the building up of public opinion on lines likely to promote a permanent peace and I am also convinced that such work is entirely in accordance with the principles underlying the suffrage movement. I was therefore anxious that it should be undertaken by the NUWSS... The Council, however, have made it clear that they were not prepared to undertake work of this kind. They passed certain resolutions, it is true, but only on the understanding that they were not to be acted upon...To my mind, this refusal on the part of the Council is not only a refusal to do the work which the moment demands, it is also a refusal to recognise one of the fundamental principles of the Suffrage Movement.[10]

These women now threw their weight behind The Hague Congress, opening an office in London, sending out applications to women to attend, and holding an organising conference on 15

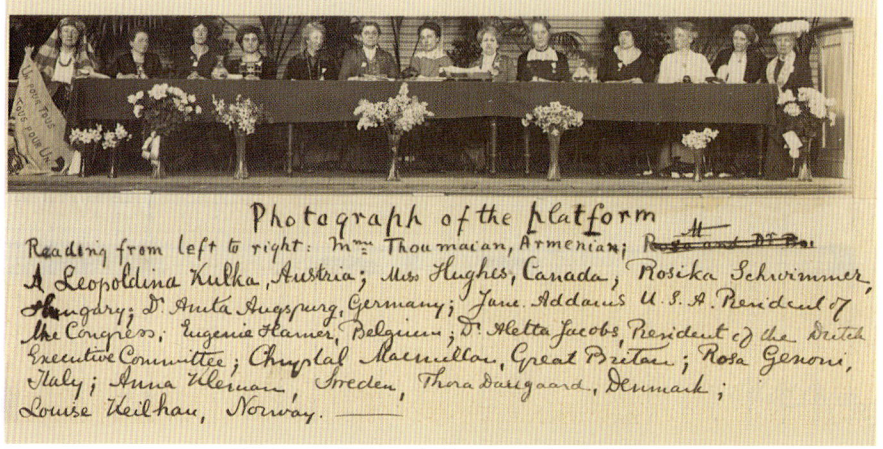

The Hague Women's Congress, April 1915

Chrystal Macmillan

Army recruiting poster, Ireland

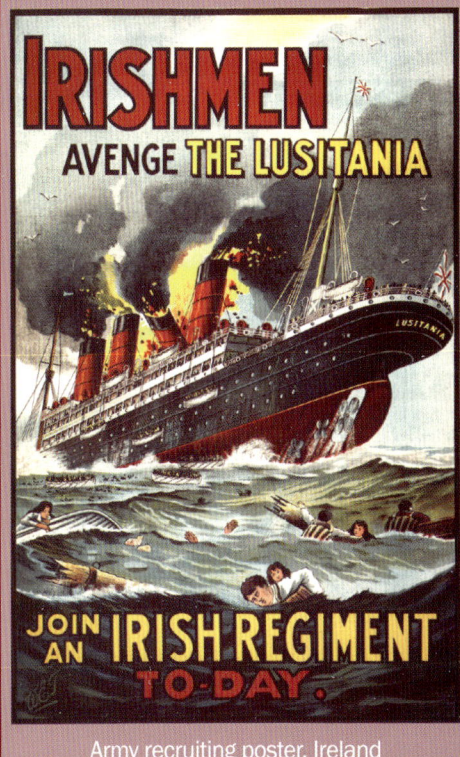

Catherine Marshall

April, attended by 450 women. They also set up local committees in a number of towns, including Manchester.

The women's campaign took place against a background of high casualties in the war on the Western Front. In March 1915, for instance, over 20,000 British, Indian and German soldiers were killed or wounded in just three days of fighting, which ended with no gain for either side. There was also a rising tide of anti-German feeling, particularly after a German submarine torpedoed and sank a British ocean liner, the *Lusitania*, on 7 May with the loss of 1,198 lives. This led to attacks by crowds on shops with German-sounding names (many of them actually Jewish) in different parts of the country, including Manchester and Salford. This was not an easy time to be seen to be reaching out to "the enemy," even in the cause of preventing another such terrible war.

In total some 180 British women applied to be delegates to the Congress, many of them well-known from their work in the suffrage or labour movement: those from Manchester included Councillor Margaret Ashton, Eva Gore Booth, Esther Roper, Sarah Dickenson and Sarah Reddish. On 19 April the Manchester Committee held a meeting in the Association Hall, Peter Street, presided over by Margaret Ashton. The guest speaker Mrs Despard moved the main resolution: "That this meeting approves of the proposed international conference of women, believing that on them, as women and non-combatants, lies the special duty to promote goodwill and a better understanding between nations; that, while not binding itself to the whole of the draft resolutions submitted by the Dutch Committee, it is in general accord with the ideal and aims set forth and pledges itself to do all in its power to promote the success of the Conference."

In her speech Mrs Despard said that as women they had not made the war and they were not allowed any part in these things which so deeply concerned them. But though women did not bear arms, they bore armies, and it was possible that at this moment they could see more clearly than men could what it was they should do. She told the audience that they were going out to The Hague to see their "sisters of all nations," and to try and understand their point of view. It was "a spirit of goodwill" that they were trying to bring forward at the conference.

Maude Royden seconded the motion, adding that the vast mass of women in the country were only waiting for a lead to perceive that peace and the women's movement went together: everywhere there was pacifism the women's movement advanced, everywhere there was militarism it went back. War was "the woman's worst enemy," she continued, and it affected the whole position of women as a sex, while there were many men to whom war was as horrible as it could be to any woman. She finished by asking, "Could they not make it impossible that these men should ever have to go to war again?"[11]

Just a week before the British women were due to travel to The Hague for the Congress the government announced that they would not issue passports and would cancel those already issued stating that "Her Majesty's government is of the opinion that at the present moment there is much inconvenience in holding a large meeting of a political nature so close to the seat of war."

Catherine Marshall went to see the Home Secretary, Reginald McKenna, and persuaded him to issue 24 passports, but it was to no avail as the Admiralty then announced that they had closed the whole of the North Sea to shipping. Fortunately, two of the British women organisers, Chrystal Macmillan and Kate Courtney, were already in Holland, having gone over to help with the arrangements for the Congress.

What was the government so afraid of? Perhaps, after the euphoria at the start of war had faded in the face of huge casualties (unprecedented in British history), they were fearful that the Congress might ignite a mood amongst the public for a negotiated peace. So, in addition to stopping them leaving the country, the government orchestrated vicious assaults in the press on the peace campaigners. The *Daily Express*, for instance, dubbed them "the

Cranquettes" and opined:

The disappointment of not seeing the bulbs in bloom, coupled with the dead seriousness with which the Cranquettes take themselves as they work in their eyrie high above a cruel laughing world, make the offices of the British Women Peace Committee a sad place now. Some day they may obtain a boat... perhaps the mothers of Scarborough and Hartlepool and the wives of the men of Mons and Neuve Chapelle and a few of the Belgians in this country who escaped from Liège and Malines with their lives and little else, will give them a parting ovation at the quay.[12]

The Congress started on 27 April with over 2,000 women delegates present. Dr Aletta Jacobs, President of the Dutch Suffrage Society, welcomed them, expressing her appreciation of the courage shown by those women who had braved all the dangers, risks and difficulties of travelling in war time from one country to another:

With mourning hearts we stand united here. We grieve for many brave young men who have lost their lives on the battlefield before attaining their full manhood; we mourn with the poor mothers bereft of their sons; with the thousands of young widows and fatherless children, and we feel that we can no longer endure in this twentieth century of civilisation that governments should tolerate brute force as the only solution of international disputes... Although our efforts may not shorten the present war there is no doubt that this pacific assemblage of so many nations will have its moral effect upon the belligerent countries...Those of us who have convened this Congress, however, have never called it a PEACE CONGRESS, but an International Congress of Women assembled to protest against war, and to suggest steps which may lead to warfare becoming an impossibility.[13]

On 30 April, whilst the Congress was still in session, the *Manchester Guardian* published a letter from the British Committee of the Women's International Committee in which they explained that, in the view of the misrepresentations of their motives, they wanted to set out the intentions and scope of the Congress. The signatories included Margaret Ashton, Margaret Bondfield, Margaret Llewellyn Davies and Helena Swanwick. They explained that:

The Congress was called by the women of Holland not with a view to demanding immediate peace or "peace at any price," but with the intention of discussing the basis on which a permanent peace may be established when this war is over, and the share which the women in each country can take in helping to build up a public opinion on these lines...

The gist of the whole programme is that war as a means of settling differences between nations is an inadmissible barbarism and madness and that some other way must needs be found. The nations must determine *now* that this is to be the last great European war. To this end resolutions have been placed on the agenda urging that arbitration or conciliation should in future take the place of war, and that the Powers should all agree to unite in bringing pressure to bear on any nation which refused to refer its case to arbitration or conciliation. It is further proposed that, the failure of secret diplomacy being now apparent, it should give way to democratic control of foreign policy...Other resolutions affirm the need for the participation of women, the mothers of the race, in those councils which will have the task of trying to rebuild our common civilisation on a surer basis.[14]

Despite the hopes raised by the Congress, there was no mediation by neutral countries between the countries locked in a murderous unending war. However, the women continued their peace efforts by setting up an International Committee of Women for Permanent Peace in a dozen countries, including Britain, where it was known as the Women's International League.

Whilst Manchester was a major centre for anti-war activity by women, even here there were sharp divisions. On 8 June 1915 Margaret Ashton resigned as Chair of the Manchester Society of Women's Suffrage Societies, while thirteen other Committee members also stood down after a meeting of the Society rejected a call for them to attempt to influence the settlement at the end of the war. In a letter to the *Manchester Guardian* Margaret Ashton explained that, whilst they had been asked to stay in office, they could not in conscience remain in office when the majority of the Society were opposed to them. They now intended to pursue the same ideals, but outside the NUWSS.

In October Margaret, now Chair of the Manchester branch of the WIL, set out in an interview with the *Manchester Guardian* the aims and objects of the League, denying that they were in favour of "a peace at any price."

It is a peaceful settlement after the war we are working for. We want to educate the nation on the real principles on which a permanent peace on just lines can be settled. Our leading object is to establish the principles of right rather than might, and of co-operation rather than conflict in national and international affairs. We lay stress on the abandonment of the theory of the balance of power, and on the reference of international differences to arbitration or conciliation. Another of our ideals is the acknowledgement of the right of men and women to determine the government of their country, and the denial of the right of annexation by conquest.[15]

The Manchester branch of the WIL was active until the end of the war. In April 1917, for instance, they protested at the bombing of the German town of Freiburg by British aeroplanes in retaliation for the sinking of British hospital ships by Germany. In a letter to the *Manchester Guardian*, signed by Margaret Ashton, Margaret Norbury, Julie Tomlinson and Anna Wilson, they said:

The British nation surely does not want wish or intend to emulate German frightfulness, to demoralise our people and degrade us in the eyes of the world. The undersigned wish to make it clear that we view with horror the dastardly sinking of hospital ships as a fresh breach of the established conventions of humanity, and, as members of the

Women's International League

(BRITISH SECTION OF THE WOMEN'S INTERNATIONAL COMMITTEE FOR PERMANENT PEACE)

12 Little College Street, Westminster, London, S.W.

MANIFESTO.

Issued by the Conference held on September 30th and October 1st, 1915, to form the organization.

Upon women as non-combatants lies a special responsibility at the present time for giving expression to the revolt of the modern mind of humanity against war. Therefore, we women of the Women's International League, assembled in conference, do band ourselves together to unite with women of all nations to demand that international co-operation between the peoples, secured by goodwill and organization, shall supersede the outworn system of warfare.

We ask that women may be given equal rights of citizenship in order that their voice may be heard in all national and international councils.

We see that alliances contracted in the hope of maintaining peace by a Balance of Power have often brought forth war, because they are an effort to balance the forces of two ever-opposed camps. We propose to work for a different kind of alliance, one which shall be a co-operation of the nations, one that shall bring forth peace. We recognize that, were such an alliance established, the healthy development, not only of individuals but of nations, would be so fostered that causes of strife would be removed before they could lead to all the various kinds of warfare, economic, social, and international.

We believe that peace is no negative thing: it is not only the condition of all fruitful work, but the result of the most strenuous and adventurous effort of mind and spirit. We dedicate our organization to the task of encouraging in ourselves and others this ceaseless effort, and of helping to mould institutions in accordance with the vital policy laid down by the International Congress of Women at The Hague, April, 1915.

WILPF manifesto

International League of Women, who, in Congress at the Hague, 1915, banded themselves together in common sisterhood to work in belligerent and neutral countries for the establishment of permanent peace, we protest against the following paragraph in a statement issued to the press, April 23, by the Secretary to the Admiralty:-

"The British government thereupon authorised prompt measures of reprisals in accordance with the announcement already referred to, and on April 14 a large squadron of British and French aeroplanes bombed ther German town of Freiburg with satisfactory results."

The "satisfactory results" included the killing of seven women and the injuring of 17 women and two children, and we cannot believe that, outside certain extremist and military circles, our fellow-countrymen wish the statement to go forth to the world that they consider it satisfactory to wreak their vengeance on German women and children for German military outrages.[16]

The Women's Peace Crusade

On 18 May 1916 the *Labour Leader* published a letter from a Miss Cahill of Lewisham who began with a question:

Are the Socialist women of Britain less mindful of their men than the women of Germany? It is now twenty-two months since war started, and as far as my knowledge goes there has not been one public demonstration against this wholesale slaughter of our menfolk.

This has not been the case with German women. They have had several ...Surely we women must make a strong effort to stay this terrible slaughter that grows in numbers every day.[17]

This letter stirred up a number of women to take action. On 10 June Helen Crawfurd and Agnes Dollan launched the Women's Peace Crusade at a conference in Glasgow, attended by 200 women, at which the main speaker was Helena Swanwick. Those present adopted a resolution appealing to all women to join in protesting against the prolongation of the war "with its horrors and senseless waste of human life." On 23 July they held a demonstration on Glasgow Green, the traditional site for meetings in the city, which a crowd of some 5,000 people attended. Margaret Ashton came up from Manchester to speak alongside Helen and Agnes and a number of other women. The *Women's Dreadnought* reported:

Not one woman was subjected to interruption. At several points the audience cheered most heartily, and in many other ways indicated their approval of a settlement of the war by negotiation...The demonstration was arranged by women, and carried through by women, who have been well led by the able enthusiastic Mrs Helen Crawfurd, who has no leisure hours that are not devoted to furthering the cause of Peace.[18]

By the summer of 1917 there were branches of the WPC in a number of towns in the north of England, but attempts to hold meetings often faced fierce, sometimes violent, opposition. Whilst in Glasgow the WPC had a good deal of popular support, and enjoyed strong links with the labour and socialist movement, in most other towns peace campaigners remained a brave but beleaguered minority, even in Manchester, where the peace movement was relatively strong.

On 10 July 1917 a group of around a hundred women met downstairs in the Clarion Café on Market Street to discuss organising a public demonstration for the WPC. This took place on 22 July in Stevenson Square, Manchester, chaired by Annot Robinson. There was a large crowd present but, according to the *Manchester Guardian,* the women's meeting was not seriously disturbed, although two smaller meetings were started in the square at the same time by those opposed to the women's meeting.

The first speaker was Margaret Ashton, who said that the meeting was intended as the beginning of a campaign in favour of negotiations for peace. The women who had planned the meeting believed that a continuation of the suffering and loss of the war was unnecessary, and that it was possible at once to open conversations and negotiations which would lead to peace, and to peace much more permanent than "a smashing victory" which would leave hatred and resentment behind it. They believed, she continued, that the peoples of all the countries engaged in the war were "ready and eager to take this course." She finished by appealing to the people to unite in demanding that the government should cease slaughter and begin to talk sense.

The meeting then passed two resolutions, the first of which called upon the Allies to publish their terms for peace at the earliest possible moment, and to repudiate explicitly the policy of indemnity and annexation. Mrs Despard spoke in support of the second resolution, which stated that the conflict was "the inevitable outcome of the present competitive system" and that a permanent peace would only be brought about by the creation of "an industrial and social order at home and abroad devoted not to individual gain but to the service of all." In her speech she said that the two qualities needed most at present were common sense and moral courage. The other speakers were Lady Barlow, Katherine Bruce Glasier, Mrs Muter Wilson, Hannah Mitchell, Agatha Watts and Emily Cox. At the end of the meeting a collection raised £7 13s 3d to cover costs.[19]

On 11 August women peace campaigners in Nelson marched through the town behind a banner which said "We Demand a Peoples Peace" and "Long Live the International." A group of young women on the march were dressed in white and carried wreaths of leaves. The march was led by Selina Cooper, very well known in the town as a socialist and suffragist. The other organisers included Gertrude Ingham and Margaret Aldersley, whose son Alex had been imprisoned as a conscientious objector. The prominent trade unionist (and future Cabinet Minister) Margaret Bondfield was also on the march.

Such was the hostility in the town to the march that no band would play for the marchers, and when they reached the meeting place they found an angry crowd of some 15,000 present, some of whom threw clods of earth at them. Margaret Bondfield tried to speak, but was drowned out by repeated choruses of "Rule Britannia" and "God save The King." After forty minutes the women abandoned the meeting. Despite this ugly experience the women still held a meeting a fortnight later in Salem School Hall at which Selina said:

I think that those who took part in the procession did something wonderful. It is one thing to come to a meeting like this: it is another thing to march through the street to be jeered and booed at. We will never forget that demonstration: I think it was something heroic...We women are in a different position from men, because the law doesn't allow us to fight, but we can go to the street corners and preach God's truth that this war should end...When the settlement comes, every woman who joined the crusade will be glad to be able to say "I joined the peace crusade."[20]

The Manchester peace campaigners attempted to hold another meeting in Stevenson Square on 8 September at which the speakers would have included Mrs Snowden, Margaret Ashton and Katherine Bruce Glasier. But, when the speakers and organisers arrived in the square, they were told by the police that the meeting was not going to be permitted.

A large hostile crowd had gathered in the square, including a number of soldiers with medals, and there were some scuffles with the police who kept the crowd moving. A Mr Pendlebury arrived with a lorry intending to oppose the meeting and was also told that he could not speak. The British Socialist Party attempted to hold a meeting in the afternoon to protest at the suppression of free speech, but this too was stopped by the police, who refused to state by which law they had stopped the meetings.

On 10 September the *Manchester Guardian* published a letter from Margaret Ashton in which she said that

Selina Cooper

British delegation at the second WILPF Congress in Zurich, 1919

The grave of George Ellison, the last British soldier to be killed

she very much regretted that the meeting had been prohibited by the police, because if the speeches had been permitted to go ahead, it would have been clear that that there was nothing "pro-German" or "unpatriotic" in their desire "to prepare the way for more stable and permanent peace in the future." She then outlined the resolution that would have been proposed:

1. Believing that war is the inevitable outcome of the present competitive system and that permanent peace can be achieved only by cooperation in enterprise, we seek to create an industrial and social order at home and abroad devoted not to industrial gain but to the service of all.

2. That this meeting urges the people of this country, together with the democracies of all countries, to demand of their governments immediate negotiations for peace on the Russian basis of no annexations and no indemnities.[21]

Research carried out by the Documenting Dissent project on "hidden histories" of dissent during the war has unearthed more examples of peace activism in the North West. Annot Robinson spoke to a meeting of 500 women in the Co-operative Hall, Burnley, for instance, on 20 September 1917: Agatha Watts spoke in Salford, Oldham and Liverpool: while Muriel Wallhead spoke in Rochdale, Southport and Barrow.

Margaret Ashton is removed from the Education Committee

Margaret Ashton's activities in the peace movement led to a personal attack on her by her fellow Manchester councillors. On 9 November the City Council voted to exclude her from the Education Committee - on which she had served for many years – and replace her with Caroline Herford, a Liberal councillor who had been elected for St Luke's ward in February 1917.

At the Council meeting Sir Thomas Shann, Chair of the Education Committee, objected to her exclusion, pointing to the work she had done over the past 13 years, and stating that, whilst he did not share her views on the war, he would be sorry to lose her as she was one of the best members on the Committee. Councillor Jackson moved an amendment to reinstate Margaret, stating that the proposal to remove her was because of her anti-war and pacifist views, views he did not share, but which had nothing to do with her position as member of the Education Committee.

The amendment was opposed by Councillor Simpson, who said that the attitude of people in public positions towards the war should be the supreme test, and that Margaret by her speeches and actions was aiding Germany. The amendment was defeated, and Margaret was therefore removed from the Committee.

There were some protests over the City Council's decision from a number of organisations. The Manchester and District Federation of Women's Suffrage Societies unanimously adopted a resolution deploring the decision, and expressing the earnest hope that the Council would reconsider, while the Central Committee of the Manchester and Salford Women Citizens' Association said that her services on the Education Committee "have been of the very greatest value." The Manchester and Salford Women's Trades Union Council praised her "unwearied efforts to promote the better training of girls in our…schools" and deplored "the assumption of the Council of a censorship of the views of its members should in Miss Ashton's case have resulted in the curtailing the usefulness of her educational work." Perhaps taken aback by the public controversy, the Council nominated Margaret for the Libraries Committee at the end of November.

Undaunted, Margaret continued her public activities. On 24 November, for instance, she distributed certificates to young people leaving the Manchester Warehousemen and Clerks' Orphan School. In her speech she said that it was far easier than it used to be to find good opportunities for girls, because there were more opportunities for them that there had ever been before. Margaret went on to say that she wished to say to the parents present particularly, that now was the moment for them to make their girls strike out new lines "for the sake of the women who are to come after." Girls no doubt made excellent clerks and typists, continued Margaret, but the time had come "when they must go forth" into newer industries. "It is well worthwhile," she concluded, "to give girls a little longer education…and to train them for higher posts."[22]

The end of the war

At the beginning of November 1918, as the German army was being driven back by the Allies following the failure of its spring offensive, the Germany navy mutinied, and then spread revolution to Berlin. On 9 November the Kaiser abdicated and a socialist government was formed which agreed an Armistice on 11 November. This came into force at 11am. In the last hours of the war 2,738 men were killed: the last British soldier to die was Private George Ellison, killed at 9.30am near Mons. Helena Swanwick later recalled her feelings on that day: "I seemed to be crying all the time inside and I had to hold myself tight."

In Manchester crowds, many of them women workers, swept into the city centre to celebrate. The *Manchester Guardian* described the scene:

…Along all the main roads into the city…work-girls poured in hundreds, gathering as they went flags and the other patriotic symbols which had been so suddenly rushed out from the obscurity of the hawker's warehouse. They clambered on town-going lurries. In Market Street one saw a cart…with seven or eight sturdy girls in overalls, cheering and flag-waving…There marched into Albert Square a procession of 300 girls headed by a small man, solemnly holding a flag…The girls – for the first crowds were mainly girls - flocked in their workclothes, shawls over heads, or in the light trousered overalls of the munition works. They shouted and cheered, breaking up now and then to do a few steps of a wild fox trot. [23]

The casualties of the war had been enormous. At least ten million soldiers had been killed, millions more had been injured, while tens of thousands of civilians had died of hunger, cold and disease. In the wake of such unprecedented death and misery there was a profound longing across Europe that this should never ever happen again. Mary Sheepshanks wrote in *Jus Suffragi* in December 1918:

Women are new to politics, but that may have advantages ... We have escaped party intrigues ... and the awe for traditional conventions, which have tied men's hands and led them to accept meekly the dictates of concessionaires, diplomats, and armament firms. We are free to approach all the mystery-making of autocrats (whether they be emperors or newspaper bosses) in a spirit of bold inquiry: we can demand information; ...we can insist on fair dealing between nation and nation. We can oppose tariff systems which create enmities in order to create profits; we can support universal disarmament, and the teaching in schools ... of sound internationalism and humanity. We can oppose the greed that masquerades as patriotism, and put the happiness and welfare of the masses before territorial or financial ambitions...[24]

The Treaty of Versailles

The Armistice was followed by a peace conference at Versailles culminating in a treaty to end the war, signed on 28 June 1919, the fifth anniversary of the murders in Sarajevo. Germany was in no position to argue over the terms; its army was prostrate, while millions of its citizens were starving. The victorious and unforgiving Allies imposed harsh conditions: Germany was forced to accept the blame for the war, had to return the provinces of Alsace-Lorraine (seized in 1870) to France, and commit itself to paying the enormous sum of 132 billion gold marks to the Allies in reparations. They were also forced to disarm and demilitarise the Rhineland.

When these terms were published in May 1919 a Women's International Peace Conference had just started in Zurich, presided over by the American peace campaigner Jane Adams, with 150 women attending from sixteen countries, including Austria and Germany. Unlike in 1915, this time a full British delegation of twenty-six women attended, including Margaret Ashton, Helena Swanwick and Ellen Wilkinson.

On the first day Jane Adams arrived from Paris with details of the treaty which filled the women with dismay and foreboding. They immediately passed a resolution:

This International Congress of Women expresses its deep regret that the terms of peace proposed at Versailles should so seriously violate the principles upon which alone a just and lasting peace can be secured, and which the democracies of the world had come to accept.

By guaranteeing the fruits of the secret treaties to the conquerors, the terms of peace tacitly sanction secret diplomacy, deny the principles of self-determination, recognize the right of the victors to the spoils of war, and create all over Europe discords and animosities, which can only lead to future wars.

By the demand for the disarmament of one set of belligerents only, the principle of justice is violated and the rule of force is continued. By the financial and economic proposals a hundred million people of this generation in the heart of Europe are condemned to poverty, disease and despair, which must result in the spread of hatred and anarchy within each nation.

With a deep sense of responsibility this Congress strongly urges the Allied and Associated Governments to accept such amendments of the Terms as shall bring the Peace into harmony with those principles first enumerated by President Wilson upon the faithful carrying out of which the honour of the Allied peoples depends.

For the next two decades the Women's International League for Peace and Freedom dedicated themselves to the task of preventing another war by urging all countries to agree an international system of conciliation and arbitration. Sadly, as we know, they failed. Just twenty years later, Europe would be at war again.

Notes

[1] Sybil Oldfield, "Mary Sheepshanks edits an internationalist suffrage monthly in wartime: Jus Suffragii 1914-19," *Women's History Review*, 12:1, 2003, pp. 120-1.

[2] *Manchester Guardian*, 3 August 1914, p. 9.

[3] Robert Roberts, *The Classic Slum* (1973) p. 186.

[4] *Manchester Guardian*, 8 August 1914, p. 14.

[5] *Manchester Guardian*, 10 August 1914, p. 8.

[6] *Manchester Guardian*, 11 November 1914, p. 3.

[7] Roberts, pp. 198-199.

[8] Roberts, p. 201.

[9] Manchester, Salford and District Women's War Interests Committee, *Women in the Labour Market during the War*, pp. 3-4.

[10] Anne Wiltsher, *Most Dangerous Women* (1985), pp. 72-73.

[11] *Manchester Guardian*, 20 April 1915, p. 10.

[12] Wiltsher, p. 85.

[13] *Report of the International Congress of Women*, The Hague, The Netherlands, April 28th to May 1st, 1915, p. 5-6. Dr Aletta Jacobs (1854-1929) was the first woman to attend a Dutch university and the first female physician in the Netherlands.

[14] *Manchester Guardian*, 30 April 1915, p. 12.

[15] *Manchester Guardian*, 27 October 1915, p. 3.

[16] *Manchester Guardian*, 25 April 1917, p. 8. The German authorities claimed that the Allied aeroplanes targeted a theatre, institutes and infirmaries. The first reprisal raid took place on 15 June 1915 when French aeroplanes bombed Karlsruhe, killing 30 people. Another reprisal raid on Karlsruhe on 22 June 1916 killed 170 people, 71 of whom were children who were killed when bombs fell on a circus tent.

[17] Wiltsher, p. 147. There were food riots in several German cities in the autumn of 1915, as women protested about the new higher price ceiling for butter and food shortages. The government responded by decreeing that no fats were to be sold on Mondays and Thursdays, no meat on Tuesdays and Fridays and no flour at week-ends. In the summer of 1916 women marched to town halls in many German towns and demanded better food supplies.

[18] Wiltsher, p. 151.

[19] *Manchester Guardian*, 23 July 1917, p. 3.

[20] Jill Liddington, *The Life and Times of a Respectable Rebel* (1984), pp. 278-280.

[21] *Manchester Guardian*, 10 September 1917, p. 8.

[22] *Manchester Guardian*, 26 November 1917, p. 3.

[23] *Manchester Guardian*, 12 November 1918, p. 7.

[24] Oldfield, p. 128.

Women in the 1920s

"Labour women have proved themselves the most magnificent fighters…"

Life in Britain never returned to the way it was before the war, despite many hoping that it would. Although women were ejected from many of the jobs they had done whilst the men were away, they still enjoyed greater freedoms, both to work and to enjoy themselves. In 1928 women finally achieved the vote on the same terms as men. New opportunities opened up but also new challenges.

Fighting for the Rights of the Unemployed

There was a short boom immediately after the end of the war, but then unemployment soared to more than two million, with many demobbed servicemen looking for work, while many women who had worked in war-related industries were unceremoniously sacked. Women who had worked in the munitions industry during the war were removed from the unemployment figures in February 1919 on the pretext that their "normal work" no longer existed, and hence they were not therefore out of work.

At the same time the government encouraged local authorities to employ ex-servicemen in preference to women. In response the National Federation of Women Workers launched a campaign to defend women's right to work in defiance of the widely promoted view that women should return home and let men have their jobs. In January 1921 Margaret Bondfield said in an interview:

All this unemployment is having a disastrous effect upon the standard of life. Simultaneously a definite effort is being made to reduce women's wages. It is driving us to despair. All the work we have done is now being threatened and whole groups of women are being driven back to such wages as were paid before the Trade Board Act of 1909. It must be an object lesson to women on the importance of organising themselves in industry, but meantime the poorly paid groups are bearing the brunt of the attack.[1]

On 11 November 1921 the Lancashire and Cheshire Federation of Trades Councils and Labour Parties held a conference to discuss the issue of unemployment. Manchester socialist and former suffragette Annot Robinson led in a deputation of unemployed women to address the delegates with one unnamed young woman, who had lost two brothers in the war, speaking movingly of the difficulty of "keeping body and soul together" on the insurance allowance of just 12 shillings a week, "I don't know what to do. No landlady will keep a girl on less than 27 shillings a week. I have kept in a straight way up to now but I am sure that 12 shillings a week cannot keep me in a straight way. And what are we going to when it stops and we have nothing?"[2]

The National Unemployed Workers' Movement (NUWM) was formed on 15 April 1921 to fight for the rights of the unemployed, adopting the slogan of "Full Work or Full Maintenance at Trade Union Rates." In the autumn of 1922 the NUWM organised their first national march with over 2,000 marchers from different parts of the country converging on London. However, there was no women's contingent on this nor on any other NUWM march in the 1920s. The movement's National Organiser Wal Hannington opposed their participation, holding a traditional view of women's role in society, despite his membership of the Communist Party, which in theory supported equality for women. Katie Loeber, who knew Hannington through her husband Ernest Kant, recalled when interviewed by Sue Bruley in 1978: "He wasn't hostile, he just didn't think of women."

In 1923 Lily Webb became the NUWM Women's Organiser. Born in 1897 in Yorkshire, Lily grew up in a working class socialist family. She started work in the mills in Ashton-under-Lyne and after seven years went to work as a bus conductress in Macclesfield. Lily joined the Communist Party in 1920 soon after its founding, as did her brother Harry. After losing her job she became active in the NUWM. In 1924 she got married to a fellow Communist, Maurice Ferguson, and they were taken on as joint full-time workers for the party, sharing one wage. Lily travelled extensively around the country as an organiser, while at the 1926 NUWM conference she successfuly moved a resolution opposing compulsory domestic service training for women and demanding other forms of industrial training and also maternity grants.

During the general election campaign in May 1929 Lily spoke in Manchester in support of the Communist candidate for Platting, Joe Vaughan, at a meeting at Burgess Street school in Harpurhey. She made a speech squarely in line with the party's election programme "Class Against Class," stating that the Communist Party was fighting Labour as well as the Conservatives and Liberals in the present election since all three parties were supporting capitalism. "We are opposing Labour on the same grounds as we are opposing Toryism and Liberalism, for if the programmes of all three parties are examined they are found to be the same." She argued that the war of 1914 had been brought about by the rivalry of the Great Powers for trade, raw materials and colonies. "In 1914 Germany was the rival, in 1929 America is the rival. The commercial rivalry is inevitably leading to a war with the United States," predicted Lily.[3]

In December 1929 Lily was elected onto the Party Central Committee at the

page 15

party's Eleventh Congress. When Maurice was sent to Moscow she joined him, and served as delegate to the Women's Section of the Communist International. On her return from the Soviet Union in 1930 the party sent her to organise amongst working women in Birmingham, where she was heavily involved in the Lucas women workers' strike in May and June 1932. In October 1932, Lily was sent to Burnley for a short time to help with the Women's National Hunger March to London, assisting the NUWM Women's Organiser Maud Brown. She seems to have ceased working full-time for the party after 1936 and lived quietly with Maurice in the countryside until their deaths, he in 1957, she in 1959.

As unemployment fell after the mid 1920s, so the activities of the NUWM diminished. However, the movement sparked back into life again in the early 1930s when unemployment soared to levels unprecedented in British history. This will be discussed in the next chapter.

Campaigns for Equality for Women

In the wake of achieving a partial victory on the issue of the vote in 1918, a number of former suffragists and suffragettes now put their energies and campaigning skills - honed in the Votes for Women agitation - into working for a greater degree of equality for women. They were assisted by the Sex Disqualification (Removal) Act, passed in 1919, which stated that people should not be disqualified "by sex or marriage from the exercise of any public function, or from being appointed to or holding any civil or judicial office or post, or from entering or assuming or carrying on any civil profession or vocation."

The first woman to be appointed a Justice of the Peace was Councillor Ada Summers, Mayor of Stalybridge, who had been elected onto the Council in 1912, making her first woman councillor in the Cheshire mill town. On taking her seat on the bench for the first time in January 1920, she said, "I have been in favour of this for many years because there are so many cases of women and children coming before the courts that can be more easily understood by women than men. I have had a great deal of experience amongst women and children, especially amongst the poorer people, in cases of this kind, and I think it will be advantageous to have ladies sitting on our magisterial benches." Only three cases were down to be heard, men charged with allowing their chimneys to catch fire. Their cases were all dismissed, while one of the defendants congratulated Mrs Summers on taking her seat.[4]

In March 1919 the National Union of Women's Suffrage Societies, the largest non-militant suffrage society, which had hundreds of branches across the country, adopted a new name: the National Union of Societies for Equal Citizenship. Mrs Fawcett retired as President and was replaced by Eleanor Rathbone, with Eve Hubback serving as General Secretary. Its leading members in Manchester included Mary Stocks and Mrs Simon. NUSEC adopted a six point programme:

1. Equal pay for equal work, involving an open field for women in industry and the professions.

2. An equal standard of sex morals as between men and women, involving a reform of the existing divorce law which condoned adultery by the husband, as well as reform of the laws dealing with solicitation and prostitution.

3. The introduction of legislation to provide pensions for civilian widows with dependent children.

4. The equalisation of the franchise and the return to Parliament of women candidates pledged to the equality programme.

5. The legal recognition of mothers as equal guardians with fathers of their children.

6. The opening of the legal profession and the magistracy to women.

In March 1928 NUSEC succeeded in persuading Manchester Education Committee to reject a proposal to sack women teachers who had got married, a common practice in many other local authorities and which the Sex Disqualification (Removal) Act did not prevent.

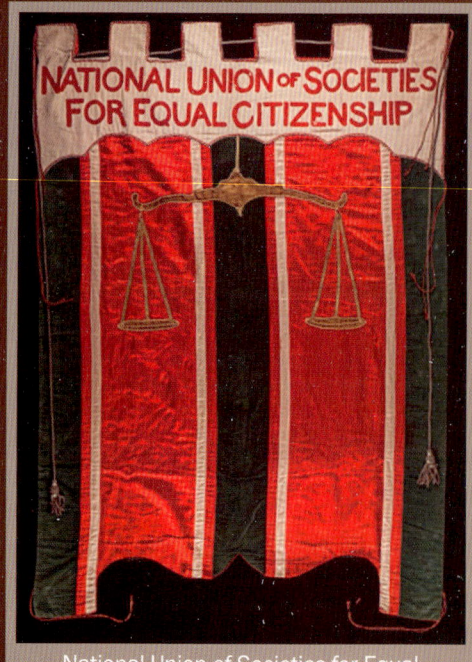

National Union of Societies for Equal Citizenship banner

Lady Rhondda (Margaret Mackworth)

Margaret Street Socialist Hall in Openshaw

Another organisation which campaigned for equality, the Open Door Council, was founded in 1926 by Lady Rhondda (Margaret Mackworth), Elizabeth Abbott, Lady Balfour and Chrystal Macmillan (who in 1924 had become one of the first women barristers). The aim of the Council was "to secure women's right to work on the same terms as men without being subject to special protections." They wanted legislation to be based on the nature of the work rather than the sex of the worker, and fought attempts to restrict women's right to work.

As well as holding meetings and conferences, the ODC also lobbied organisations, sending delegations to the Labour Party, TUC and ILP. In February 1929 Elizabeth Abbott debated on the radio with Dr Marion Phillips, Chief Woman Officer of the Labour Party, on the question of protective legislation for women: Elizabeth opposed special treatment for women, while Marion supported it.

A Manchester branch of the ODC was established at a meeting in October 1928, presided over by Councillor Hannah Mitchell. Olive Aldridge from London (who had been an organiser for the Manchester Women's Trade Union Council between 1904 and 1914 and served as a nurse in Serbia during the First World War) addressed the meeting on the question of labour conditions, comparing the position of women with that of men. She referred to the proposed Factory Act and said that it was urgent that voters should be informed of the harmful limitation of women's work which would probably be proposed. The lowering of the status and pay of women would not benefit men, Olive argued, but would tend to "depress the condition of men's employment." The party which had the wisdom to be sincere in assisting women to secure equal status, pay and opportunities, she contended, would capture women voters. Hannah was elected President of the new branch, with Mrs Williamson Forrester acting as Secretary. Within a year they had 76 members.[5]

In July 1929 members of the British ODC went to an international gathering in Berlin, attended by delegates from 18 countries, which set up an International Open Door Council with Crystal Macmillan as President. Vera Brittain wrote that "the future activities of the Open Door Council should be well worth watching both by enemies and friends. Its courage and tenacity are unrivalled amongst women's organisations and its vital committee appears to have inherited something of the fire and energy which animated the WSPU in the days of Pankhurst."[6]

In November 1929 the Manchester branch of the ODC held a meeting at which the main speaker was Mrs Le Sueur from London who spoke about the founding of the Open Door International. Mrs Aldridge, national organiser of the ODC also spoke, while Mrs Forrester presided over the meeting.

Women in Local Government

Although women had had the right to be elected as city and town councillors since 1907, only a small number had made their way into Council chambers prior to 1914. After 1919 a greater number of women began to be elected, although they never approached anything like 50 per cent of the total. In Manchester Margaret Ashton, elected in 1908, and Caroline Herford, elected in 1917, were joined by a number of other women, including Annie Lee, Hannah Mitchell and Ellen Wilkinson.

Annie Lee

Annie was Secretary of the Openshaw Socialist Society (formed in the 1890s), which became the most active socialist society in Manchester. In 1907 the Society built a Socialist Hall on Margaret Street, where they organised many social, political and educational activities, as well as running a Socialist Sunday School. This urged young people to "love learning" and look forward "to the day when all men and women will be free citizens of one fatherland and live together as brothers and sisters in peace and righteousness."

In 1918 Annie took her first public office when she was elected to the Poor Law Board of Guardians. Amongst her actions on behalf of the poor was to fight successfully for a man who had had all his teeth removed to be given the cost of a set of false teeth. She argued, "What's the use of granting a man a food order if he has no teeth to eat the food with? He can't live on slops alone." She said she did not see herself as a "Poor Law Guardian" but a "Guardian of the Poor."

In November 1919 Annie was elected as a councillor for Gorton South, one of two Labour Party women elected that year. She remained on the Council until June 1936, serving on the Education, Watch and General and Parliamentary Committees. According to Stella Davies, Annie was "eternally dressed in a navy blue costume and a black felt hat and wore sensible flat-heeled shoes."

Annie believed in equal pay and equal opportunities for women, and campaigned forcefully for this whenever possible. In December 1926 at a meeting of the Education Committee, for instance, she objected to the fact that male attendance officers were being paid more than female attendance officers, which she described as a "gross injustice." Annie tried to get the appointments postponed for six months whilst the matter was looked into, but her motion was not seconded.

In January 1928 Annie supported Councillor Shena Simon at a meeting of the Education Committee when she moved that it was advisable that the Committee should adopt "a consistent attitude towards the work of married women." Councillor Simon pointed out that for six years they had had a policy of sacking women teachers who got married, but had then retained some in special circumstances. In seconding the motion Annie said that it was only when they came to the teaching profession they found such a bar existed: a private employer would not discharge a woman because she had got married. She declared that the only point that the Committee should consider in regard to the employment of married teacher was whether she was "capable of doing the job." In the end the motion was not discussed, but postponed to a future meeting.[7]

In November 1929, at a meeting of the Board of Guardians, Annie attempted unsuccessfully to overturn the compulsory resignation of a nurse who had got married. She said that she resented any Board of which she was a member dismissing a woman because she had got married, for it was an interference with the principle that a woman should be able to earn her own living after marriage in the job for which she was most suited:

Everybody knows there is an ever higher standard demanded in regard to the training of nurses as in the teaching profession...After much difficulty the City Council have been brought round to the view that marriage ought not to debar teachers from carrying on their profession, and we ought not to tell nurses that if they want to continue in their profession they must refrain from marrying. The only thing we ought to ask them when engaging them is whether they are qualified to do the work required.[8]

Annie was not afraid to stand her ground in defence of her socialist principles. She sparked off stormy scenes at a meeting of the Board of Guardians in October 1929 when she attempted to raise a case of hardship. The Chair, Hugh Fay, said that the matter was one for the General Purposes Committee, but Annie persisted with her point amidst cries of "Chair!" and "Sit down!" She was then joined by other Labour members, who also shouted at the Chair. "In the turmoil no one paid any special attention to choice of language and all engaged in personalities," reported a journalist. Eventually Annie's amendment was put amidst the confusion - and lost.

After subsiding for a few minutes, the uproar re-ignited, even more heatedly, after Annie gave notice of a motion to revert to the scale of outdoor relief which had prevailed before November 1927. When Hugh Fay ruled that it could not be heard, Labour members began shouting at him, and then at each other across the room, so much so that Annie eventually turned to her fellow Labour Guardian, George Hall, and asked him, "for goodness' sake, be quiet." According to the *Manchester Guardian*, "By this time the whole of the Board were embroiled in the disturbance, each one shouting at the other without seeming to know what he was shouting about." Finally Hugh Fay adjourned the meeting.

There were similar scenes a week later when Annie tried to move a resolution on the scales of relief, which, after more bad-tempered shouting and Annie accusing the Liberals and Conservatives of trying to exclude the press, was defeated. The following month's meeting was peaceful and Hall apologised to the Chair.[9]

Annie resigned from the Public Assistance Committee in December 1931 because of a recent decision by the Council that councillors should no longer administer poor relief in their own wards. She said that the people had the right to the services of the representatives they themselves elected, particularly in times of distress when they were forced to apply for public relief.

When she became a member of the Council's Watch Committee (which oversaw the police), Annie persuaded her colleagues to appoint a woman police surgeon, Nesta Roberts, to deal with sexual assaults on women and children, the first such appointment in the country. When it appeared in April 1933 that the Committee was quietly trying to dispense with this appointment she objected forcibly until her fellow councillors agreed that Nesta's services would be retained.[10]

Annie died on 25 October 1945: her brother Joseph, whom she had looked after for many years, died the same day in the same hospital. In its obituary the *Manchester Guardian* quoted Councillor Wright Robinson: "No member of the City Council was held in higher respect or esteem for she was a woman who had the strongest convictions and stood them fearlessly. Nothing could shake her on such matters as Sabbath observance and opposition to Sunday games or equal pay for men and women." Councillor Mabel Tylecote spoke of Annie's determined support of feminism, and the inspiration which her leadership in her earlier years had obviously given to a great many women.[11]

SISTER, ARE THERE TO BE MORE GRAVES?

OVER YOU GO!

KEEP THE HOME FIRES BURNING

Cover illustrations from *The Labour Woman*. From top: February, 1927; November, 1927; April, 1929 and July 1926.

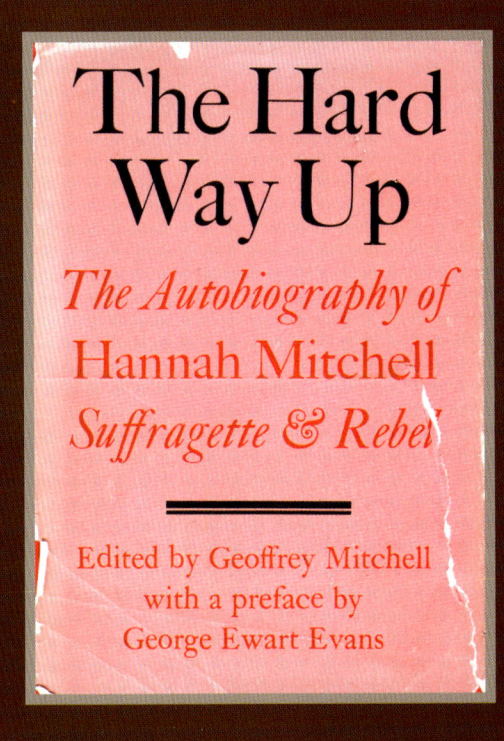

Hannah Mitchell

Hannah Webster was born in 1871 in Derbyshire. In the years before the First World War she was an active socialist in the Independent Labour Party, and also an active suffragette, firstly in the Women's Social and Political Union, and later in the Women's Freedom League. She married a fellow socialist, Gibbon Mitchell, whom she had met whilst living in Bolton.

During the war Hannah remained true to her socialist beliefs and opposed the conflict, joining the No Conscription Fellowship and Women's International League. Her son decided that he could not fight, applied to the Conscientious Objectors Tribunal, and, to his mother's great relief, was granted exemption. Instead of being sent to the trenches he was sent to work on tree felling in Ireland, surviving an accident and also Spanish Flu, which he caught in the largely forgotten pandemic of 1918.

Hannah's neighbours in Newton Heath, like families up and down the land, had lost sons and fathers. She reflected that:
Men came home full of hope for the brave new world which was promised them by the politicians, but which turned out to be even worse than the pre-war England we had tried to imbue with the ideals of Socialism. A short-sighted peace settlement soon threw the country into such a morass of unemployment and misery as we had never seen before. Philp Snowden had prophesied in the House that the war would leave the rich richer, and the poor poorer. Perhaps we socialists were less disappointed than most, or perhaps less surprised.[12]

Hannah's local branch of the ILP reformed soon after the war ended, and she recommitted herself to the socialist cause in the party which she felt was her "spiritual home." Her branch carried out a good deal of propaganda, funded by regular dances and whist-drives, and brought well-known speakers into the district whom Hannah looked after, including A J Cook, the miners' leader. However, she refused to join the Women's Section of the Labour Party, set up in 1918 to replace the Women's Labour League, brusquely dismissing them as "a permanent Social Committee, or Official cake-maker to the Labour Party."

In 1921 the ILP nominated her as a candidate for Manchester Council for the Newton Heath ward, but she was promptly turned down by the Labour Party, because, according to Hannah, she was too well-known as a keen feminist and, as they put it, "not amenable to discipline." The ILP nominated her again two years later, but again the Labour Party turned her down, preferring a man who thought that being a councillor would help his business, but as it turned out, he went bankrupt within six months and had to step down from the Council.

Once again the ILP nominated Hannah, now offering to guarantee the expenses of the election. Reluctantly the Labour Party accepted Hannah as a candidate, fearing that otherwise they might lose the seat after the fiasco with the insolvent candidate. Her ILP comrades flocked to help her, holding open-air meetings on every street corner, knocking on every door, and driving electors to the poll. She won the seat by a narrow margin of 82 votes, increasing this in later contests.

Hannah remained a member of the Council until 1935, serving on a number of Committees. She found that being on the Parks Committee was a disappointment, recalling that to her "parks meant trees, flowers and rest: to my male colleagues they seemed to mean football, bowling greens and tennis courts." By contrast the Libraries Committee was much more to her liking: "Here I found my varied reading stood me in good stead. Being able to read quickly and sum up the contents of a book in a short time, I felt I was really useful on the Book Selection Committee…"

Hannah served on the Baths Committee, which established public wash houses in working class areas, including Newton Heath, where it meant that "a family wash could be done in a couple of hours…a real public service greatly appreciated by women." Sitting on the Public Assistance Committee (which replaced the Board of Guardians in 1930) she had many battles with her fellow councillors over the relief of the poor.

In August 1929 Hannah spoke during a debate at the meeting of the Council on a proposal advanced by Mrs Simon, a Liberal, that 450 houses to be built in Newton Heath should have a downstairs bathroom, no parlour and three bedrooms. Hannah publicly disagreed with her Labour colleagues, George Hall and Annie Lee, who wanted houses with parlours, and supported the motion. She said that she risked "being called a reactionary," but living in Newton Heath she felt that she knew what kind of house was required: where working-class families lived in parloured houses, they let off rooms to pay the rent. It was no use, Hannah continued, having parlours for children to study in if they could not afford to pay for the gas. Even the present government would not give a bigger subsidy, and in spite of ideals they had to meet "the immediate pressing need." Mrs Simon's proposal went through.[13]

Looking back, Hannah considered that the two outstanding events of her time on the Council were the purchase of the Wythenshawe Estate and the building of Central Library. After leaving the Council Hannah continued to work as a magistrate. She died on 22 October 1956. In its obituary the *Manchester Guardian* described her as "one of the oldest and most respected members of the labour movement in the North of England and a pioneering member of the suffragist campaign."

Hannah had been working on her autobiography for many years, but it was never accepted for publication in her lifetime, although some extracts did appear in the ILP newspaper *Labour's Northern Voice* in the 1950s. After her death the manuscript was found amongst her papers, and was finally published by faber and faber in 1968 under the title *The Hard Way Up*, with an introduction by her grandson Geoffrey Mitchell. It is now considered a classic account of a working class woman's personal and political emancipation.

Ellen Wilkinson

Ellen Wilkinson was born on 18 October 1891 at 41 Coral Street, Adwick. After working as a pupil teacher for a time, she gained a scholarship to read history at the University of Manchester, a very considerable achievement in this era for a working class young woman.

Ellen was already involved in the socialist movement, having joined the ILP at the age of 16 after hearing a speech made by Katherine Glasier, one of the leading women socialists of the day. At college she was Secretary of the Fabian Society, and also active in the Manchester Society for Women's Suffrage. On leaving university Ellen got a job as the Manchester organiser for the National Union of Women's Suffrage Societies, and was then employed by the National Union of Distributive & Allied Workers to organise the Co-operative employees, the first woman organiser to work for the union.

Like many ILP members, Ellen opposed the First World War and supported the No Conscription Fellowship. In 1917 she joined the Women's International League.

In August 1920 the Manchester branch of the Guild Socialists sent Ellen to attend the Unity Convention in London, which brought together a number of existing socialist organisations to form the Communist Party of Great Britain. Like many young socialists of that era she was inspired by the Soviet Union, a state which appeared to be in the hands of the working class, and joined the Communist Party later that year. (Until 1924 it was possible to belong to both the Labour Party and the Communist Party).

On 27th April 1921 the National Conference of Labour Women held its annual meeting in Milton Hall, Manchester, attended by 500 delegates and presided over by Margaret Bondfield. No doubt motivated by her visit to Ireland in October 1920 as part of a WIL delegation, Ellen moved a motion condemning the government's "anarchical methods of government in Ireland," urging it to withdraw all armed forces, to "place the responsibility for maintaining order on Irish localities" and "to provide for the immediate election by proportional representation of an entirely open constituent assembly, charged to work out at the earliest possible moment without limitation or fetters, whatever constitution for Ireland the Irish people desire."

She said that future historians would find it most difficult to understand the incredible apathy now displayed by British people with regard to what was going on in Ireland. One could visit a smiling, happy village in Ireland one day, and go there again a little later and find that it looked like a cartoon from Belgium. More and more women were being arrested, Ellen said, and when arrested they were not taken to women's prisons but to men's prisons, and often kept there five or six weeks without any woman to attend them.[14]

In the summer of 1921 Ellen attended the founding conference of the Red International of Labour Unions in Moscow, spending five weeks in the Soviet Union. On her return she gave an interview to the *Manchester Guardian* about her impressions and experiences, particular in relation to the famine in the Volga where millions were at risk of starvation:

While not wishing to minimise the gravity of the situation, she declared that much that had been written about it could not be relied upon. The Soviet Government, she said, was not, as had been asserted, panic-stricken by the crisis, but had set up adequate machinery for distributing relief when it arrived and for getting food from other parts of Russia to the famine area...

The reason for the incorrect newspaper stories is that most of the journalists who are writing about Russia are outside Russia. They are not allowed to come into it, and so they write fanciful yarns from the frontier towns...The whole of the relief arrangements were being organised by the military machine, with Trotsky at its head, and the military machine was the most efficient organisation in Russia...The stories of fundamental differences between Lenin and Trotsky were nonsense...they worked together on the affectionate terms of men who had been through a lot together. She noticed, however, that Lenin looked very tired. It was obvious that that he was overworked.[15]

In November 1923 Ellen was elected as a Councillor for Gorton South, standing on behalf of the Gorton United Trades

Ellen Wilkinson

Labour Party women's conference

and Labour Council. Her friend Stella Davies said her small figure, generally dressed in green and her hatless flaming hair made "a bright spot of colour" in the "drab Gorton streets."

One of her first acts was to propose a motion at the full Council meeting asking the Works for Unemployed Special Committee to report on what relief works could be provided for unemployed women. This was an issue that Ellen pursued whilst she was on the Council. In May 1924, for instance, both she and Councillor Mary Welch complained at a Council meeting about the difficulties they were encountering in securing schemes for the relief of 8,000 unemployed women in Manchester. It was not enough, said Ellen, merely for the Council to say it had not the power, it ought to take measures to get power. Ellen remained on the Council until 1926.

In the general election held in December 1923 Ellen stood as the Labour Party candidate for Ashton-under-Lyne. Reviewing the contest, the *Manchester Guardian* described Ellen as having "Communistic views," although she had been officially endorsed by the local and national Labour Party. The report noted that her candidacy "has not been hailed with universal delight," and that the Secretary and President of the local miners' union preferred to support the Liberal Party. In her campaign Ellen attacked the Tories and the Liberals as "the outdated creeds of the last century." She came third in the poll, gaining 28.7% of the vote. Nationally a minority Labour government came to power in January 1924, with Ramsay Macdonald as the first Labour Prime Minister, but it lasted just nine months.

In September 1924 Ellen issued a statement explaining that she had left the Communist Party two months previously because of its indiscriminate attacks on the Labour government, and because "its exclusive and dictatorial methods made impossible the formation of a real left wing amongst the progressive elements in the trade unions and Labour Party." She denied that her resignation had anything to do with wanting to stand for parliament.

In the general election held the following month Ellen was elected as a Labour MP for Middlesbrough East, although the minority Labour government was defeated. For a time she was the only woman on the Labour benches in the Commons. Ellen returned to her native city on 9 November 1924 to speak to an audience of several thousand, who crowded into a cinema in Moston. She made them laugh by telling them that "it was comforting to think that they had

THE LABOUR WOMAN

Edited by DR. MARION PHILLIPS

A MONTHLY JOURNAL FOR WORKING WOMEN

PRINCIPAL CONTENTS for January, 1922

SIR ALFRED MOND ASKS THE BABIES TO PAY FOR THE WAR

SPECIAL ARTICLES ON LABOUR WOMEN ABROAD
THE LIFE OF A WAITRESS
THE COMMON SENSE OF REPARATIONS
WOMEN JURORS
HOW THE GOVERNMENT IS GOING TO ECONOMISE

TO SPREAD KNOWLEDGE: SELL LITERATURE. SOME WAYS OF DOING IT

SERIAL STORY

COMPETITION FOR YOUNG PEOPLE
STORY FOR LITTLE ONES

POLITICAL ORGANISATION, NOTES FROM THE WASHHOUSE, ETC.

Vol. X   PRICE TWOPENCE   No. 1
SUBSCRIPTION (with postage), THREE SHILLINGS ANNUALLY

that monument of consistency and stability, Winston Churchill, in charge of the nation's finances." She attacked the capitalist system, asserting that wages had declined in value since 1900, whilst "the wealth in the hands of the few had grown." In the next Budget they would see the tax of the rich man reduced, leaving the poor "the victims of the profiteer." They could not feed their children or build houses so long as this "financial octopus" had hold of them. "This is not a fight for party," she finished to the sound of cheering, "but a crusade for the freedom of the human race."[16]

Ellen made her first speech in the Commons on 3 March 1925 in which she criticised the working conditions for workers employed at the British Empire exhibition. On 29 June 1926, whilst Ellen was speaking during a debate on the Coal Mines Bill, she produced a rope used by miners in Somerset, who had to haul the coal tubs themselves as the roads were too narrow for horses or ponies.

After the defeat of the General Strike in 1926 she went to the United States to raise money for the families of miners who remained on strike until the autumn. In 1927 Ellen co-authored *A Workers' History of the Great Strike* with Frank Horrabin and Raymond Postgate: in 1929 she wrote a novel called *Clash* set against the backdrop of the General Strike. During the second Labour administration (1929-1931) she worked for Susan Lawrence, Parliamentary Secretary to the Minister of Health, Arthur Greenwood. Ellen lost her seat in the general election of October 1931, but returned to the Commons in November 1935, this time as MP for Jarrow.

Charis Frankenburg and Mary Stocks, pioneers of birth control

Mary Stocks and Charis Frankenburg founded the Mothers' Clinic for Birth Control in Salford which opened in 1926.

Mary Brinton was born in 1891, attended St Paul's Girls' School in Hammersmith (where the music teacher was the composer Gustav Holst), and then the London School of Economics. In 1913 she married the philosopher, John Stocks. During the war she taught at the London School of Economics, and after the war the couple moved to Oxford, where she taught at Somerville and Lady Margaret Hall. In the early 1920s Mary Stocks was joint editor with Eve Hubback of a feminist publication, *The Woman's Leader*.

At the end of 1924 they moved to Manchester after John was offered a professorship in philosophy at the University. The couple were soon drawn into the middle-class cultural life of the city, which revolved around the University, the *Manchester Guardian*, and the University Settlement at the Round House on Every Street, Ancoats, where Mary directed a number of plays, including five she had written herself. She also worked for the WEA, travelling out to villages to give history lectures.

Mary had known the birth control pioneer Marie Stopes since 1918, having met her at Oxford soon after the publication of Stopes's book *Married Love*, which caused a public sensation because of its straightforward discussion of birth control. In 1921 Marie opened the word's first birth control clinic in London, and in 1924 a group of progressive women and men founded the Society for the Provision of Birth Control Clinics to campaign for municipal clinics in other parts of the country.

Charis Barnett was born in London in 1895. Her family were Christians, her father having converted from Judaism. She too attended St Paul's Girls' School, and then went to Somerville College. During the First World War Charis trained as a midwife and served in France. In 1918 she married her cousin, Sydney Frankenburg, who died in 1935 from an infection resulting from a war wound.

Charis was active in a plethora of local philanthropic organisations, including the Manchester and Salford Women's Citizens' Association and the Salford branch of the Midwives Institute. She also campaigned on maternal mortality, which led her to take up the issue of birth control to prevent what she described as "the tragedy of and waste of exhausted mothers and dead infants." As she recalled in her autobiography *Not

Mary Stocks

Old, Madam, Vintage:
Having read the books of Dr. Marie Stopes...and profited by her expertise – we had four children spaced exactly as intended – I wrote in the autumn of 1925 to ask her to tell me of someone near Manchester who might be interested in helping me to set up a Birth Control Clinic. She suggested Mrs. John Stocks. I recognised her as Mary Brinton, whom I had known at St Paul's, and immediately wrote asking if she would help. She agreed enthusiastically and on October 23rd, we collected a few friends and formed a committee, electing her as Chairman and me as Hon. Organizing Secretary. In the following weeks we made enquiries, visited the Stopes and Wolverhampton Clinics, enlisted Mrs. Robert Burrows as Honorary Treasurer, a brave doctor and a nurse-midwife, Dr. Olive Gimson, and Sister Pulford, and acquired two rooms over a little baker's shop in Greengate.[17]

Mary was a Socialist, while Charis was a Tory, but they worked together for a cause in which they both believed. On 26 January 1926 campaigners organised a conference on Maternal Mortality in Manchester at which the dangers to women's health of excessive pregnancies were highlighted by a number of speakers. This attracted considerable comment in the press, and Charis used this opportunity to write a letter to the *Manchester Guardian*, referring to cases in which women had had numerous pregnancies and lost their babies through miscarriage or still-birth. She was frank about the desperate

Charis Frankenburg

measures that some women resorted to when facing an unwanted child:

> Surely no human being can read of these authenticated cases and say that instruction in birth control is not a crying need. Each of these tragedies had its own special factor, but it is fairly obvious that there is one predisposing cause – the rapid pregnancies of the mother, which left her no time to recover her strength, or to give adequate care to the child that she already had. There is a subsidiary cause even more pitiful. These helpless mothers, who know that another pregnancy means probable death to the baby in their arms – themselves and their danger they rarely think of – spend incredible sums on illegal and fearsome operations, on violent drugs, and some of them throw themselves downstairs or under motor-lorries in a last effort to get rid of the child that should never been conceived.[18]

Charis finished her letter by explaining that the Ministry of Health would not allow doctors at infant welfare centres to give advice on contraception, and consequently a Committee had been set up to establish a Mothers' Clinic for Birth Control which had taken premises at 161 Greengate, where only married mothers with one child would be seen, except at the doctor's discretion. The cost would be one shilling: she appealed for donations to support the clinic.

This was a controversial initiative. Even before the clinic opened there were objections, particularly from the Catholic church, which held a protest meeting. Writing in 1962 Mary Stocks recalled:

> The climate of opinion, generally, was cold towards birth control. In Salford it was, to say the least of it, frigid. We had to face intense opposition from the Roman Catholic clergy. Mrs. Frankenburg and I were singled out for special obloquy. We were "the kind of women who visited matinees and sat with cigarettes between their painted lips." The image was in one respect comforting, for we envisaged ourselves as rather dowdy social workers. And our clinic was described as being reached through a "stinking entry." This was a little hard for the stink was in fact merely the homely smell of good hot meat pies. But the location of the clinic through the shop made attendance easy for shy mothers – and they came, the shy and the not so shy.

> But it was not only the Roman Catholic clergy who regarded us as less than respectable. The Church of England stood aloof. The medical profession, with one or two shining exceptions, was to say the least, unhelpful. By many people "birth control" seemed to be regarded as a dirty word. Moreover strange misconceptions were afoot. We were abortionists. We helped unmarried women to evade the consequences of their sins. We recommended practices which caused cancer. In fact, of course, we did none of these things; but it took quite a lot of public speaking to explain that we didn't. And that perhaps was the most inspiring part of the work.[19]

The Manchester, Salford and District Mothers' Clinic for Birth Control opened its doors for the first time on 1 March 1926, holding clinics twice-weekly. On that first day some 19 women attended. The *Manchester Guardian* reported that "yesterday afternoon a number of poor mothers of varying ages, having generally children with them, were climbing the stairs to the two rooms."

In their first annual report the clinic revealed that they had given advice to 423 women, and that there had been 319 repeat visits. Many women had first heard about the clinic because of the protest meeting, and whilst most of the women attending the clinic had come from Salford or Manchester, others had come from further afield, some from as far away as Scotland. They also noted that a considerable number of women had come to the clinic expecting to be given abortions, and had to be advised that this was illegal. Over a quarter of the women who attended had had previous abortions or miscarriages. The clinic later moved from its small rooms to the Greengate Hospital and Open Air School at 123 Greengate, and then in May 1939 opened new premises at 70 Upper Brook Street, Manchester.

At the start of the Second World War, Charis invited the staff and children of Greengate Hospital and Open Air School to take up residence at her home, Oughtrington Hall, near Lymm in Cheshire.

Manchester WIL delegation to Ireland

The WIL continued its work after the war, both in Britain and abroad, driven by a group of women who had been sickened by the slaughter during the First World War, and were determined to prevent it ever happening again. A second international meeting was held in Zurich in 1919, and a third in Vienna in 1921.

Manchester had a very active WIL branch which in the course of 1920 became increasingly concerned about what was being done by the British armed forces in Ireland. In the 1918 general election the Irish Republican party Sinn Fein won a majority of the Irish constituencies but, in line with their policy, refused to take their seats at Westminster. Instead in January 1919 they set up an Irish Parliament in Dublin, called Dáil Éireann, and proclaimed the Irish Republic. The British government refused to recognise Irish independence and poured in troops to Ireland. These soon clashed with the Republic's armed forces, the Irish Republican Army, whose activities were coordinated by Michael Collins. Determined to suppress the Republic, the British government augmented its army with irregular forces known as the "Black and Tans," which used increasingly brutal methods of official "reprisals." In September 1920, for instance, British forces set fire to the town of Balbriggan after two policemen had been shot.

At the beginning of October the Manchester branch of WIL made a public appeal for £500 to enable them to send "a mission of representative women" to Ireland to investigate what was really happening there. The delegation of ten women, whose members included Margaret Ashton, Agatha Watts, Annot Robinson, Ellen Wilkinson and Helena Swanwick, departed a few days later, visiting as many towns as they could. Helena took many photographs of the devastated areas, and on her return had them made into lantern slides for use in lectures given by the women.

Back in Manchester the women spoke about what they had found at a packed public meeting in the Free Trade Hall on 18th October, presided over by Mrs Muter Wilson, a former suffragist in the North of England Society. Dr Catherine Chisholm (the first woman to be accepted by the University of Manchester as a medical student) said that they had gone to Ireland, not because they hoped to solve the problem, which they knew was difficult, but because they felt that things were going on in Ireland which English people did not know about, and of which many English newspapers contained no record. They felt that if these things were told to the people a volume of public opinion could be created, which would help even the present and intolerant government to take steps. She herself had visited the North-East of Ireland where people told her, "Whatever party you belong to, we are glad you have come. It is time the English people realised what is happening."

Helena Swanwick, who had visited Dublin, said that the Irish had chosen their own government, and must therefore be allowed to be ruled by it. Dail Eireann, she continued, was the only government which had moral authority and the consent of the people and England was now holding down Ireland by "force, fraud and terrorism." She went on to say that the English people were being fed lies about the state of affairs, and these lies were responsible for the "dullness of the English conscience on the subject." In the first nine months of the year, for instance, there had been 62 murders by the police, the army and the "Black and Tans."

Ellen Wilkinson had visited Limerick, Galway and West Clare. She observed that Mr Lloyd George had declared it inconceivable that British soldiers would attack without provocation, but she told the meeting of her visit to a farm which had been raided by the military. During the raid the women had been forced up a mountain road in bare feet, and a young woman beaten with rifle-butts by soldiers in an attempt to make her tell where her brothers, who were Sinn Feiners, were. In another village she was told of a man (not a Sinn Feiner) who had been shot and wounded by soldiers and then flung by them "still shrieking" into the middle of a burning house. She accused the British government of "deliberately crushing the economic life of the Irish people." At the end of proceedings the meeting passed a resolution urging the British government to set free all Irish political prisoners, and to offer a truce during which "all armed force should be withdrawn and the keeping of order placed in the hands of local elected bodies."[20]

After Manchester the women spoke at many meetings around Britain, sometimes sharing platforms with members of a recent Quaker delegation to Ireland. They showed the lantern slides which, as Helena Swanwick later recalled, did more than any words could have done to convince audiences of what was being done in their name:

Audiences that were cool before, broke into cries and groans when they saw the ruined homes of Tuam, the roofless cottages of a whole street in Balbriggan, the wrecked shops and creameries and town halls of Cork and Mallow, the paralysed old women being rescued. "Why it's like Belgium!" was the commonest of all remarks one heard.[21]

Two of the women on the delegation - Annot Robinson and Ellen Wilkinson - also travelled to the United States in December 1920 to give evidence to the Villard Commission, which was investigating what was happening in Ireland. The British government had refused to allow members of the Commission to visit Ireland, so the hearings were held in Washington.

At the hearing the two women disclosed that, whilst they had no difficulty in obtaining passports from the Foreign Office, when they had applied for travel visas to Mr Wells, the United States Consul in Manchester, he had initially refused, telling them that they were "not encouraging inquiries in America into the state of affairs in Ireland." Eventually, after personally lobbying the United States embassy in London, and asking some influential friends to intervene, the two women were granted visas to cross the Atlantic, provided that they promised not to address meetings, engage in propaganda or grant interviews.

In her evidence to the Commission Annot Robinson explained that the British public was largely unaware of the true situation in Ireland, because:

...the reports of shootings and reprisals and all that have been published only on one side. On that side you have the great mass of official papers and official reports, which make the people think that the shootings and the atrocities in Ireland have been wholly unprovoked. And that, of course, is very harmful on the attitude of the people.[22]

Ellen Wilkinson made a similar point in her testimony about the refusal of many British people to believe in the reality of the terror being wreaked in Ireland by British forces:

And while I think that English opinion at last is being aroused, they say that our own boys are being killed, and we don't think that our own boys would do the terrible things that you say they do, anyway. And we say that when you get these boys together and talk to them and fill up their minds with the idea that every Irishman is a murderer, you bring a war psychology and then you get the atmosphere that makes it possible for these things to be done. And that is why I say you must blame the Government rather than the boys who are doing these things.[23]

After another seven months of brutal violence, a truce between the British government and the Irish Republican

Workers clearing rubble on St Patrick's street following the burning of Cork, 1920

Peacemakers' Pilgrimage, 1926

government came into force on 11 July 1921, followed by negotiations which led to a treaty and the establishment of the Irish Free State in 26 counties of Ireland in December 1922. The other six counties of Ireland had already become Northern Ireland with its own Unionist-dominated Parliament.

The Peacemakers' Pilgrimage

In the summer of 1926 the WIL, together with numerous other organisations, organised a Peacemakers' Pilgrimage from many parts of the country to London, very much modelled on the 1913 Suffragist Pilgrimage. The aim was to raise the question of peace and international arbitration which, the organisers felt, was not being addressed with enough urgency, even by the League of Nations. They said that they wanted to show the government that "this country wants law not war," and, that in particular, they wished the British government to accept compulsory arbitration in international disputes by the League of Nations, something that 17 other countries, including Germany and Russia, had already agreed to.

The Chair of the organising committee was Mrs Eleanor Acland, a leading member of the Women's National Liberal Federation, while the Treasurer was Emmeline Pethick-Lawrence, the former suffragette. In March Emmeline addressed a conference of 50 societies in Manchester, which included the Society of Friends, the League of Nations Union, the St Joan's Social and Political Alliance and the Women's Co-operative Guild, all of which agreed to support the Pilgrimage.

The Women's Citizen Association organised a further meeting on 12 April at the Ancoats Settlement, Manchester to rally support for the Pilgrimage. Mrs Muter Wilson reviewed the history of attempts to bring about international arbitration of disputes between countries from William Penn to the League of Nations. She said that there was no greater mistake than to suppose that the mere existence of the League would in itself secure peace. She thought that the Locarno Pact might have made peace, had it been followed by a disarmament conference, but although 17 countries had signed the arbitration clause, Britain had not yet done so. She believed that the Pilgrimage was "a force to be reckoned with."[24]

Seven Peacemakers' Pilgrimage marches set out in May (coinciding with the General Strike incidentally), holding hundreds of meetings along the way. On 17 June there was a procession in Manchester in support of the Pilgrimage, which gathered in Stevenson Square at 5pm, and then marched with pennons and banners to the Cathedral, which was packed to the doors. After being addressed by the Dean the procession went to Platt Fields, where a crowd of 2,500 heard speeches from Councillor Mary Welch, Cecile Matheson and finally Kate Courtney, who said that the Pilgrimage was an expression of "an aspiration to permanent peace," an aspiration which, she believed, filled the mind of almost every man and woman in the country.

The 3,000 marchers on the Pilgrimage reached London in mid-June. They held a final mass procession on 19 June ending in Hyde Park, where there were 22 platforms for the speakers, who included Dame Millicent Fawcett, Margaret Bondfield, Ellen Wilkinson, Emmeline Pethick-Lawrence and Evelyn Sharp. At the end of the meeting bugles were sounded, and a resolution was put urging the government to agree to submit all international disputes to arbitration or conciliation.

On 16 July a delegation from the Pilgrimage went to the Foreign Office, where they met Sir Austen Chamberlain. Mrs Acland presented him with a report from the Pilgrimage, and emphasised that its object was not merely to speak of the desirability of world peace, but to put before their countrymen the need for England to "throw the full weight of its immense prestige" on the side of international law "as against international anarchy." Chamberlain replied to the women with emollient diplomatic speak, assuring them that the government was reviewing "the whole question of arbitration in international affairs."

The Pilgrimage inspired the Manchester branch of the WIL to arrange a series of meetings on the theme of peace in July 1927 in a number of villages and towns in Lancashire and Cheshire, including Bollington, Newton-le-Willows, Stockport, Whaley Bridge, and Wilmslow. The speakers at these meetings included Councillor Mary Welch, Mrs Muter Wilson and Dr Vipont Brown.

Crowds in Albert Square and Piccadilly during the General Strike

The General Strike, May 1926

The General Strike was the most significant British labour dispute of the twentieth century, a nationwide strike called by the Trades Union Congress in support of a million miners, locked out by the mine owners after they refused to accept the imposition of cuts in pay and longer working hours.

The strike began on 3 May 1926 and was unilaterally called off on 12 May by the TUC on the basis of a meaningless memorandum, with no guarantees from the Tory government of either fair treatment for the miners or no victimisation for returning strikers. Abandoned by the TUC the miners' strike continued until November, when it ended in bitter defeat.

From the beginning of 1926 many expected that the dispute between the mine owners and miners would end in a strike. *Labour Woman,* the journal for women members of the Labour Party, commented in an editorial on the implications for women:

The next few months must decide whether it is to be peace or war in the mining industry; and if the mine-owners' solution prevails, it will mean less wages, longer hours and still more unemployment. Against that, Labour, politically and industrially united, must prepare its forces to fight to the end. This is a struggle of quite as much importance to women as to men. All must join together to keep the home fires burning, for it means no less: lower wages for miners will lead with absolute certainty to a reduction in wages for all. Food, boots, clothes, fuel, light and rent – all of these have to be bought, and with lower wages, how is the housewife going to meet the needs?[25]

On 30 January 130 delegates attended a conference in Gorton, Manchester of the South East Lancashire Labour Women's Advisory Council at which the women agreed to co-operate with the Lancashire and Cheshire Miners' Association in spreading propaganda among women on the coal crisis.

The annual labour movement May Day march in Manchester took place on Saturday 1 May. Undeterred by the rain, thousands paraded from Ardwick Green to Belle Vue under "dripping banners" and "rain sodden umbrellas" as the *Manchester Guardian* reported:

Men and women in gleaming mackintoshes and wearing the red and yellow favours of the Labour party: delegates from trade unions following in dignity behind their banners: Communists with broad ribbons across their shoulders - a splash of colour in the drab train: hatless youths carrying literature: groups of decorated children: a quarter-mile procession crawling like a spiritless snake along the dampness of Hyde Road …The banners of the trade unions were varied by those of other groups, ranging from a sober 'Stand by the Miners' to the appeal of the Communists – 'Don't shoot the Workers'.[26]

After the procession a meeting took place in the Great Hall at Belle Vue at which, in the midst of the speeches, Joe Compton, MP, announced that "the trade unions of the country have decided to call a general strike." After a moment's hush the audience broke into cheers with Communists waving their red streamers, and hats being thrown into the air. Every reference from the platform to "the coming fight" and every appeal to "stand by the miners" was received with cheers and applause. The meeting finished by unanimously agreeing a resolution in support of the miners which ended, "We declare that this struggle is not for the miners alone. He who is not for the miners is against the working class."

The strike began at midnight on Monday 3 May. As the deadline approached railway workers, tramwaymen, carters, dockers, power enginemen, printers, iron and steel workers, vehicle builders and builders all announced their intention to strike work. The Electrical Trades Union, which had its headquarters in Manchester, issued an instruction to its branches to take joint action "along with any other section of men who have ceased work on transport, printing, engineering and steel production."

Councillor Mellor, Secretary of the Manchester and Salford Trades and Labour Council, gave assurances that every effort would be made to co-operate with local authorities in ensuring the safety of food supplies and other essential services. The trade unions set up a central committee to run the strike in the North West. The Secretary was J A Webb from the Transport and General Workers Union, whose members would be crucial to the success or failure of the strike. At midnight, for instance more than 5,000 Manchester tramwaymen held a mass meeting in the Co-operative Hall, Downing Street, Ardwick at which there was a solid vote in favour of striking. The power for the trams was cut off at 2am.

Stella Davies, a member of Gorton Labour Party, vividly recalled the first day of the strike in her book *North Country Bred*:

The mill chimneys ceased to smoke and the wheels ceased to turn. Over Gorton, Openshaw, Clayton, Newton Heath and Collyhurst the air grew clearer; the hills which ring the east of Manchester could be seen with an unusual sharpness across the intervening river valleys. The pavements and even the roads were crowded with pedestrians and the drivers of private cars offered lifts with surprising generosity.[27]

The largest group of women workers in the country - the textile and silk workers in Cheshire, Lancashire and Yorkshire - were not called out on strike by the TUC. However, a number of women did get involved in supporting the strike, although in a traditional way. Stella Davies, for instance, visited a local railway station with other members of the Labour Party Women's Section, taking tea and sandwiches. The trains had been stopped, although there were attempts to help the service going using student strike-breakers:

The pickets were steady responsible men who, as the occasional train drew into the station, regarded with interest and much amusement the efforts of the amateurs to bring the engine to stop at the right place and not over-shoot the platform. 'Now you know,' they said to one discomforted youth, who had taken the train right through the station, 'any fool can start a train. When you've learned to stop it where you want it, you can join the Union'. The men who formed the bulk of the Labour Party and trade unions were not given to striking heroic attitudes nor had they high falutin' ideas about themselves. There was, however, during this week of the General Strike, a sense of pride in the disciplined response of organised labour to their collective decision.[28]

On Sunday 9 May there was a large rally in support of the strike in Platt Fields park, Manchester. Two brass bands made up of striking tramway workers led the procession into the park. Stella Davies described it as "a large orderly crowd and the presence of many women and children with sandwiches and bottles of milk made it seem almost like a picnic....the speakers exhorted the strikers to keep quiet, stay at home, and offer no provocation..." The speakers, (which included Mary Quaile, who was on the General Council of the TUC) addressed the crowd from three platforms. A report on the meeting sent to the TUC estimated that there were at least 20,000 people present.

On Wednesday 12 May thousands of striking tramwaymen defied threats from their employer and refused to return to work, mustering instead at their depots at noon and marching into the city centre. The procession from Hyde Road depot was a half-mile long, led by the tramway band and miners carrying lamps. But, even as the procession set off, the General Strike was coming to an end.

The government had refused to negotiate with the TUC. Instead there had been secret meetings between the TUC and Sir Herbert Samuel, who had previously chaired a Commission into the coal industry, but was acting as an individual, and not as an envoy from the government. The miners' leader, A J Cook, only found about these meetings when he was told by Mary Quaile. On the basis of a memorandum prepared by Samuel the TUC went to Downing Street and called off the strike, even though this document had already been rejected by the miners' leaders. It was no less than a complete surrender.

Stella Davies later described how the news was heard in Manchester:

In the course of the afternoon while I was on my round of the picket-stations, the news came through. The end of the strike had been announced on the radio as an 'unconditional surrender'. The picketers could not at first believe it. They would wait until they heard from their own headquarters before they left their post and I left them, still picketing, to rush home and sit before the wireless. No comfortable words came from the BBC. The official governmental line was that the Samuel Memorandum was not binding upon them, being merely a recommendation, its terms were not, in the event, put into operation.[29]

In the aftermath of the end of the strike, there was a bitter row at the Manchester Board of Guardians' meeting on 19 May between the Chair and Councillor Annie Lee, who was attempting to second a motion. She accused the Chair of the Board of moving a vote whilst she was still on her feet, and declined to withdraw, exclaiming "you can send for the police." The Chair replied, "I will not send for the police, but I will send for the porter." Other Labour members then gathered around Annie, one of them exclaiming, "He will have to take her over my dead body." The situation was resolved when Annie was given another three minutes to complete her observations.

Annie subsequently wrote to the *Manchester Guardian* on behalf of the Labour Guardians' Group, explaining that the background to the "scene" (as the newspaper had described it in its report) was the fact that the Board had sent 600 beds to the docks for the use of strike-breakers. The decision was taken by a small advisory body without the knowledge of the Board. Annie said the Labour Guardians considered this action to be "an unconstitutional way of conducting the business of an important representative body" and, coupled with the reduction of strikers' relief by 10 shillings, was placing the Board "in the position of taking sides in a dispute."[30]

Abandoned, the miners and their families faced months on strike with few resources. On 20 May the miners' leader A J Cook asked Labour Party women if it was possible to get a committee together to

Miners' children pictured in *Labour Woman*

run a Flag Day for the wives and children of the million locked-out miners. The women reacted immediately, holding their first meeting within 24 hours at which they set up the Women's Committee for the Relief of Miners' Wives and Children, which now took over the mammoth task of collecting funds for relief.

The Chair of the Committee was Ellen Wilkinson, MP, while others involved included Susan Lawrence, MP, Marion Phillips (the Labour Party's Women's Officer) and the journalist Evelyn Sharp. They were given premises by the Parliamentary Labour Party in London where volunteers helped with clerical work, while supporters donated typewriters and even cars.

In a statement they said that they were appealing on behalf of miners' wives and children "who are now in desperate straits. Long periods of short time and low wages have exhausted their resources, and the lock-out finds them facing actual starvation. Some of the mining valleys, owing to the bad trade of the last few years are now practically famine areas."

The Committee immediately sent out a circular to every Labour Party, Trades Council, Women's Section and Women's Co-operative Guild asking them to form Local Relief Committees. Over the next few weeks they arranged tours of miners' choirs and speakers such as Ellen Wilkinson, and also set up a scheme for collecting donations at cinemas and music halls. They raised £6,500 within five days, but said that they needed "hundreds times as much and next week we are all out to get it. And above all, we rely on the Labour women to help us to get it." In August Ellen Wilkinson went to the United States in August with Ben Tillett and others to raise money, speaking in New York and Pennsylvania.

The North Western District of the Labour Party Women's Advisory Council reported that:

... the Advisory Councils and the Sections have been engaged in the relief work in connection with the coal lock-out. In the districts, other than coalfields, the Sections have been raising money, holding pound days, etc, to help the distress, particularly to help Bolton, where the Guardians have behaved so inhumanly. Sections have also arranged adoptions of children for the duration, and have made clothes and collected boots, clogs etc.[31]

Finally, as the autumn leaves fell, the mining communities were forced back to work on the mine owners' terms. *Labour Woman* summed up the struggle in an editorial, finding hope even in bitter defeat:

Helping our Fellow Members

For nearly five months the whole strength of the Labour women of Great Britain has been thrown into the struggle against the coalowners and the Government. Outside the coalfields every effort possible has been made to collect money and clothes and food for the mining areas. Within the coalfields the women have slaved day or night to carry out the work of relief as well as gather whatever assistance they could for the national and local funds. It has been a truly heroic effort, and it has shown no weakening in spite of every force that can be brought to bear by hardship and injustice to break down their spirit. In this epic of Labour and Capital, this most terrible example of class war, Labour women have proved themselves the most magnificent fighters. They have not fought by words, but by deeds.[32]

WOMEN AND THE MINERS' LOCK-OUT

The Story of the Women's Committee for the Relief of the Miners' Wives and Children

By

MARION PHILLIPS
D.Sc. Econ., Chief Woman Officer of the Labour Party

The Labour Publishing Company, Limited
38 Great Ormond Street, London, W.C. 1

Notes

[1] *Manchester Guardian*, 17 February 1921, p. 7.

[2] *Manchester Guardian*, 12 November 1921, p. 6.

[3] *Manchester Guardian*, 25 May 1929, p. 16. The constituency was won by the Labour candidate, J R Clynes, with 22,969 votes (57.9%). Joe Vaughan got 401 votes (1 %).

[4] *Manchester Guardian*, 1 January 1920, p. 7.

[5] *Manchester Guardian*, 31 October 1928, p. 13. *Manchester Guardian*, 1 August 1929, p. 8.

[6] *Manchester Guardian*, 1 August 1929, p. 8.

[7] *Manchester Guardian*, 24 January 1928, p. 13.

[8] *Manchester Guardian*, 28 November 1929, p. 15.

[9] *Manchester Guardian*, 24 October 1929, p. 13. *Manchester Guardian*, 30 October 1929, p. 13.

[10] *Manchester Guardian*, 6 April 1933, p. 11.

[11] *Manchester Guardian*, 26 October 1945, p. 8.

[12] Hannah Mitchell, *The Hard Way Up*, pp. 187-188.

[13] *Manchester Guardian*, 8 August 1929, p. 6.

[14] *Manchester Guardian*, 28 April 1921, p. 8.

[15] *Manchester Guardian*, 10 August 1921, p. 6.

[16] *Manchester Guardian*, 10 November 1924, p. 9.

[17] Charis Frankenburg, *Not Old, Madam, Vintage* (1975), p. 134.

[18] *Manchester Guardian*, 13 February 1926, p. 14.

[19] Mary Stocks, "Greengate Clinic," in *Women Talking: An Anthology From The Guardian's Women's Page*, edited by Mary Stott (1987) pp. 6-7.

[20] *Manchester Guardian*, 19 October 1920, p. 12.

[21] Helena Swanwick, *I Have Been Young* (1935), p. 136.

[22] *American Commission on Conditions in Ireland* (1921), p. 573.

[23] *American Commission on Conditions in Ireland* (1921), p. 596.

[24] *Manchester Guardian*, 13 April 1920, p. 14.

[25] *Labour Woman*, 1 February 1926, p. 24.

[26] *Manchester Guardian*, 3 May 1926, p. 11.

[27] Stella Davies, *North Country Bred* (1963), p. 229.

[28] Stella Davies *North Country Bred* (1963), p. 230.

[29] Stella Davies, *North Country Bred* (1963), p. 231.

[30] *Manchester Guardian*, 21 May 1926, p. 11.

[31] *Labour Woman*, 1 September 1926, p. 140.

[32] *Labour Woman*, 1 October 1926, p. 152.

Women in the 1930s

"Work Work Work, We want work, And an end to the Means Test..."

The Wall Street Crash of October 1929 led to a recession which was turned into a slump as governments around the world followed orthodox economic theory by slashing their spending and cutting wages and benefits, thereby sending their economies into a downward death spiral. In Britain unemployment rose remorselessly with northern industrial area such as Lancashire being particularly hard-hit. In the face of desperation and poverty the National Unemployed Workers' Movement (NUWM) reignited its campaigning with protests and Hunger Marches, which now included women marchers for the first time. At the same time there was a bitter struggle on the streets against the British Union of Fascists, while in 1936 workers organised in support of the Spanish Republic with women from Manchester going to Spain as volunteer nurses. Finally, at the end of the decade Britain found itself at war again with Germany.

Marching for the Rights of the Unemployed

By 1933 unemployment in Britain reached over three million. In their history of the decade *Britain in the Thirties* Noreen Branson and Margot Heinemann write starkly about what this meant:

The early thirties...faced large sections of British people with a virtual breakdown of the whole economic system under which they lived. One of the richest countries in the world was patently unable to provide great numbers of its people with any way of making a living. Not only the working-class movement, but growing great numbers of middle class and professional people suffered from a sense of insecurity.[1]

Unemployment was not spread evenly across the country, but was sharply regional in its effects, concentrated in the traditional industrial areas in the north of England, Wales and Scotland. In Lancashire, for instance, on 7 July 1930 there were 321,506 unemployed men and 204,776 unemployed women, equating to some 27% of the workforce, the highest total in England.

The NUWM revived its campaigning, and in this decade there was greater participation by women. At the 1929 annual conference Mrs Youle from the Sheffield branch successfully moved a motion that all branches with more than 20 women members should establish women's sections, and that a national women's department should be established. By 1931 five women's section were functioning in the north of England which sent delegates to the annual conference: Barnsley, Bradford, Hucknall, Leeds, and Wombwell, There were also a number of active women's sections in Lancashire.

Maud Brown was appointed as the national women's organiser. She came from a working-class family in North London and had worked as a post office sorter. She was active in the Labour Party in Tottenham in the mid 1920s, and had started volunteering at the NUWM offices in London in the late 1920s. In his history of the NUWM *We Refuse to Starve in Silence - a history of the National Unemployed Workers' Movement, 1920-46* Richard Croucher says that the appointment of Maud Brown "marked the beginning of a rapid and qualitative improvement in the movement's work among women." She brought fresh energy, and a new approach, and was remembered by her fellow activists as a "terrific fighter" and

Unemployed women looking for work

being "afraid of nothing and nobody." Unlike most of the other leading members of the NUWM, Maud was not a member of the Communist Party, and was apparently unpaid for her work.

The 1930 National Hunger March

In March 1930 the NUWM organised a third National Hunger March to London, made up of twelve contingents which converged on the capital from different parts of the country. For the first time there was a women's contingent drawn from Lancashire and Yorkshire, most likely as a result of the new approach to work amongst women being driven by Maud Brown.

According to Margaret McCarthy, who was on the march, it was difficult to find volunteers, perhaps because of the length of time women would be away from home or, for women with children, the eternal problem of child-care.

Margaret, who was single, was a weaver from Accrington and a Young Communist League member. Rose Smith from Mansfield was an experienced political activist. Born in 1891, she joined the Social Democratic Federation and then the Communist party in 1922. She qualified as a teacher, but when she got married in 1916 to Albert Smith she lost her job, a fate suffered by many women teachers. Instead she went to work in munitions where she became a trade union official. She later worked in the leather trade, making gloves. In 1928 Rose became a full time organiser for the Communist Party and in the 1929 general election she stood for the party in Mansfield, but only gathered a few hundred votes. She separated from her husband and went to live in Burnley.

Also on the march was Mrs Youle, who had four children and was married to an NUWM organiser. Another marcher was a woman from Nelson had worked in the weaving sheds for 40 years: in her knapsack she had a pair of clogs which she wore on alternate days. Most of the women were married, although there were two young women aged 15 on the march, one of whom was a cotton worker from Oldham, another was from Bradford. The marchers carried a number of banners, one of which read "Burnley Weavers – Seven Hours Day and Damn Eight Looms" whilst another proclaimed "Under Fed, Under-Clad, Under the Labour Government."

After a rally in Burnley the eight Lancashire women went by rail to Bradford where they met up with a larger group of Yorkshire women. On 21 April they set off together on foot towards London. By the time they reached Leeds at tea-time most of them needed iodine and ointments for their feet, which is not surprising, as they were wearing artificial silk stockings and low open shoes, hardly suitable footwear for a walk of many miles. The local Communist Party gave them tea and accommodation, and an appeal was made for walking-sticks and haversacks, pointing to a surprising lack of preparation for the march.

At Wakefield they spent the night in the Union House and then, now numbering some thirty in total, marched to Barnsley, where they were greeted by the Reverend David Allott, a Labour councillor. He had arranged for them to have tea and to spend the night in a schoolroom at Worsbrough Common, tucked up with blankets provided by the Public Assistance Committee.

On reaching Sheffield (now carrying haversacks and walking-sticks) they denied that they were footsore, telling the press "Our feet are as strong as our hearts" and sang songs. After mounting a demonstration in the city centre, they were given tea at the Communist Institute on Attercliffe Road. They had intended to stay overnight in the Fir Vale Workhouse, but refused to accept being treated as "casuals" ie being bathed and searched before being admitted, and walked out. The women then tramped the streets in the rain in an exhausted state, accompanied by the police, until 5.30am when they were given shelter and breakfast in the Communist Institute, sleeping fully clothed on floors and in chairs.

On Saturday morning Mary McCarthy, an unemployed weaver from Burnley, addressed a meeting at Barker's Pool, telling the crowd that they were marching on London to demonstrate against the government. Rose Smith told the *Sheffield Independent* that they had had a prior undertaking that they would not be treated as "casuals," and had refused to enter the workhouse or the House of Help. After the meeting the women went to the headquarters of the Unemployed Workers' Union where, as previously arranged, they were put on a motor-coach to Luton.

Here things improved a good deal. The women were put up overnight in the King Street Congregational School, given a good breakfast, and then resumed their march - except for one woman from Bradford, who had sprained her ankle and had to be sent home. Rose Smith told a reporter:

We are demonstrating against unemployment. We know it is bound to

Women marchers, 1932

Women marchers led by Maud Brown, 1932

First aid for feet on the 1934 march

get worse. There is no cure for it under capitalism. It is a mistake to think we object to the introduction of machinery. We don't, but we think it should lighten people's labour, but under the capitalism competitive system it does not mean that, it means speeding up. In the textile industry they are introducing the eight-loom system, and women operatives tell me that, though it is impossible for women to work that way, they are doing it.

At St Albans the local Trades and Labour Council arranged accommodation for them: the following day they set off towards Barnet. As they neared London Maud Brown told the *Manchester Guardian* that they were angry at the attitude of the Labour Party in the towns that they had passed through. "They are out to boycott us. They know we are protesting at the attitude of the government and many of them will have nothing to do with us." At Barnet they boarded a bus to Finchley, and then marched to Islington.

On arrival the women marchers were met by the London Women's Action Committee, who presented them with red scarves, while at the rally in Hyde Park the veteran socialist Charlotte Despard gave Maud Brown some red tulips. After the rally the women stayed on in London for a while. They attempted to see the trade unionist Margaret Bondfield, now Minister for Labour, but she refused to meet them, most likely because both the Labour government and the TUC viewed the NUWM with deep suspicion owing to its links with the Communist Party.

In the wake of the march Maud Brown and other women worked hard to recruit women into the NUWM, holding meetings outside Labour Exchanges, and building up sizeable women's sections, especially in the north where large numbers of women were out of work. The largest branch was in Sheffield, which by early 1935 had 300 members.

At the NUWM conference in Bradford in February 1931 Maud Brown moved a motion on "The Task Amongst Unemployed Women," which called for proper facilities at Labour Exchanges for unemployed women and crèches for women who were looking for work. It also called for equal benefits and equal pay for women, as well as improved maternity and child welfare services.

However, Maud faced an uphill struggle to get men in NUWM branches to take agitational work amongst unemployed women seriously, and had to send out a number of circulars upbraiding NUWM branches for their attitude to women members. She complained that "no serious attention is being taken of the correspondence sent out by the women's committee…the comrades fail to understand the importance of work among women."

The economic crisis was accompanied by a political crisis. In the summer of 1931 there was a run on the pound after the May Committee predicted that the government would be in deficit within months, and recommended drastic cuts in government spending eg reducing the salaries of civil servants, teachers, the police etc. The government looked for loans to cope, but the banks demanded reductions in unemployment benefits. The Labour Cabinet split over the issue, and on 24 August the government resigned. The Prime Minister Ramsay MacDonald and the Chancellor Philip Snowden now deserted their party, joining forces with the Tories and Liberals to form a so-called "National Government", with MacDonald remaining as Prime Minister. He was denounced as a traitor by most Labour Party members and expelled from the party.

This crisis was followed by a general election in October 1931 which produced a landslide victory for the National Government (in reality a Tory government), while Labour was reduced to a rump of just 50 MPs. This result gave the new government the green light to impose drastic cuts in public sector salaries and to savagely reduce support for the unemployed. Women were singled out for attack when the Anomalies Act - introduced by Margaret Bondfield earlier in the year - came into force in October. This Act removed tens of thousands of married women from the register, refusing them the right to register as unemployed in their own right.

Further misery followed on 5 October when the government increased contributions to the Unemployed Insurance Scheme, and on 12 November when it introduced a "Household Means Test" for workers who had already received 26 weeks of benefit. The Means Test (as it quickly became known) removed hundreds of thousands of people from statutory benefit who were now classified as "transitional" claimants and placed under the jurisdiction of the new Public Assistance Committees.

PAC officials assessed the weekly income of households as a whole, including those still lucky enough to be in work, and the amount by which it was greater than Poor Law Relief was then deducted from the claimant's benefit. In many cases it forced the unemployed to live off the wages of the employed members of the household. Not surprisingly the Means Test was the most detested of all government measures, and the misery and humiliation it created has lingered long in popular memory. There were many protests around the country in the autumn of 1931 with marches in Salford and Manchester, for instance, being attacked by the police and the leaders arrested, including Eddie Frow, co-founder with his wife Ruth of the Working Class Movement Library in the 1950s.

The 1932 Hunger March

The fourth National Hunger March organised by the NUWM took place in October 1932: its prime aim was to draw public attention to the Means Test and an across-the board cut in benefits of ten per cent. As in 1930, the march had no official support from the Labour Party or the trade union movement at national level, which still viewed the NUWM with suspicion. Local parties and trade unions, however, were more supportive with assistance and accommodation.

This time the women's contingent numbered about forty, mostly cotton weavers aged from 16 to 62. They set out from Burnley on 9 October where they had been joined by some women from Scotland. Their route south took them through Todmorden, Halifax, Huddersfield, Barnsley, Rotherham, Worksop, Alfreton, Derby, Burton-on-Trent, Coalville, Hinckley, Rugby, Northampton, Wolverton, Dunstable, St Albans and London, which they reached on 27 October.

The women included Maggie Nelson, a weaver from Blackburn, who was remembered by Marion Henery, one of the Scottish marchers, as a "very strong personality" who was very successful at addressing street meeting at which she "... won their hearts and got great collections." Maggie acted as "postwoman" for the contingent, picking up their letters on the way. She was separated from her husband, and therefore left her three children with friends whilst she was on this march and later marches in 1934 and 1936. Maud Brown and Lily Webb led the contingent which chanted slogans such as:

Work Work Work
We want work
And an end to the Means Test
Slave camps and the rest

Their reception was mixed. Lily Webb recalled that in some areas:
**Reception committees awaited us in the towns we stayed in for the night, and often they marched out to meet us and carry our packs. Sometimes they came out with bands and banners and always a great crowd awaited us...
The Reception Committees organised by the NUWM were many times joined by other working class organisations, including the Co-operative Women's Guilds, whose numbers played a big part in the number of the reception centres, especially in the collection of funds, etc, as did women members of the CP, ILP, TUs etc.**[2]

Women marchers, 1932

In other towns the women faced indifference, or even hostility. At Burton-on-Trent, for instance, they discovered on arrival that the letter from the National March Council, sent to the town's Trades Council and Labour Party asking for help, had been handed to the police, who had been informed that the trade union movement would not be associated in any way with the march. As previously the women refused to enter the workhouse under "casual conditions" and instead processed through the streets, held several meetings, and then marched to the workhouse, accompanied by a crowd of several thousand. Maud Brown led the negotiations with the workhouse managers, who eventually climbed down, and the women marched triumphantly into the building.

On 23 October they had to halt at Bletchley, instead of their intended destination of Leighton Buzzard, because of the incessant rain and floods in the area. The next day they walked for seven hours in the pouring rain to reach Luton. After this miserable experience when they got to Dunstable the local ILP branch sent a motor-coach to pick them up and gave them lunch before the women set off again.

At St Albans Mrs Caisley from Burnley addressed a meeting in the market place, telling the crowd that she was 63 years of age and had been a cotton operative for 45 years: "I have 16 children, 23 grandchildren and one great-grandchild." Here the local Trades Council, as in 1930, was supportive, organising an evening social, accommodation, food, boot repairs – and, perhaps most welcome of all, baths!

There was also a women's contingent on the NUWM march from South Wales. Dora Cox recalled how the women marchers grew in confidence through their experiences and the discussions en route, so that by the end a number of them, who had never before spoken in public, were able to articulate the impact of unemployment on themselves and their families.

The women's contingent reached London on 26 October - along with the other contingents - numbering several thousand marchers in all. Their intention was to present a petition, signed by a million people, against the Means Test and the cuts in benefits. The authorities had prepared well for what was to come, drafting in thousands of provincial police and recruiting special constables to augment the Metropolitan police. Extraordinarily, they even announced that the Coldstream Guards were being held in readiness.

The following day a crowd numbering around 100,000 gathered in Hyde Park to welcome the marchers. The speakers included Lily Webb, and very helpfully for historians, a certain Police Sergeant Davies took shorthand notes on her speech, which have been retained in the Home Office files. Lily said:

Comrades and fellow marchers, as one of the leaders of the women hunger marchers who have marched from Burnley to London, I want first of all to convey the greetings of women marchers to London workers. I also want to thank you on behalf of the women marchers for the magnificent reception that you have accorded to us women marchers, not only on entering London yesterday but at this great demonstration this afternoon. I have never had the honour of speaking in London before to-day, and I can say, comrades, I have never seen a sight like this in the working class movement, outside Russia. I am proud to be able to speak at this meeting. We are fighting to abolish the rotten Means Test. The workers all over the country are fighting against it as they never fought against anything before, and we will continue to fight until it is smashed. The way we have been received in London has made us more determined than ever. The reception by the Islington workers exceeded all our expectations. Whilst our immediate task is to fight the Means Test, we shall follow the example of the workers of Soviet Russia, to be able to abolish unemployment. Before we can overthrow unemployment we shall have to overthrow capitalism.[3]

When the crowd in the park was attacked by mounted police some of those assembled tore up a number of the railings to defend themselves. There was fighting between the crowd and the police in the park, and also in the streets nearby, with a number of shop windows being smashed. In the end the police were forced to give way due to the numbers doing battle with them, and the NUWM contingents eventually marched out of the park unhindered, according to Wal Hannington's account.

By February 1933 the NUWM claimed to have 100,000 members organised in 349 branches, while there were 34 women's sections. There was no national march in 1933, instead there were a number of regional ones. In early September there was an NUWM march from London to the TUC meeting in Brighton, which included a women's contingent.

The issue of hunger and malnutrition came to the fore as families struggled, and failed, to live on the meagre benefits on offer. In November 1933 the British Medical Association published a minimum healthy diet, the cost of which, the NUWM pointed out, was beyond the reach of many unemployed families. The NUWM women's department led the work on this issue with Maud Brown writing a pamphlet, *Stop This Starvation of Mother and Child*. In this she described the price of unemployment being paid by women:

Upon the shoulders of the unemployed women and the wives of unemployed men the heaviest burdens have always been placed. The woman industrial worker is unable, during pregnancy, to find anyone willing to employ her because of her condition, whilst at the same time pregnancy is not regarded as a basis of a claim for national Health benefit. Thus at the period of her greatest need the expectant mother is made to suffer additional hardship. The new Unemployment Act will certainly increase the rate at which unemployed workers are falling into arrears, and thereby being robbed of the benefits which they have already paid for.[4]

She argued for a rapid increase in clinics, welfare centres and maternity hospitals, which would bring down the high death-rate amongst mothers and babies, as well as providing work for unemployed building workers. Maud ended with a rallying cry:

We urge all workers to unite against… the Unemployment Act, against the Health Insurance Act, which penalises the wives of unemployed men. Demand free milk and meals for nursing and expectant mothers!.. We must demand that the rent and coals allowances shall be continued. We must … demand that every Borough and County Council shall put into operation work schemes at trade union rates of wages, for the provision of clinics, welfare centres and maternity hospitals… Workers of all shades of political opinion! The mothers of Britain call upon you to save them from this tragedy of maternal suffering.[5]

The 1934 Hunger March

In December 1933 the NUWM held a Congress of Action in an attempt to build a united front which led to a proposal for another national Hunger March to London. The main demands were the abolition of the Means Test, restoration of the ten per cent cut in benefits, a seven hour working day, and work at trade union rates.

Maud Brown was one of the organising secretaries of the National Congress and

March Council, while the NUWM tried to gather wider support for this march, seeking unity with the Labour Party and the Independent Labour Party in the fight against unemployment and fascism. The marchers set off in January 1934, numbering about 700.

The women's contingent started from Derby on 12 February, numbering 48, many wearing red berets and red dresses. By the time it got to London on 22 February it was 70 strong. En route they enjoyed a good deal of support from Labour Party women's sections and the Women's Co-operative Guilds, more so it seems than in previous years. When they left Barnet they were accompanied by foot and mounted police. The South Wales marchers numbered about 20 women, again led by Dora Cox. They arrived in Chiswick on 23 February, and marched down the Great West Road, led by a band, with the women sporting smart red berets.

On 24 February there was a large conference in Bermondsey Town Hall - the National Council of Action - which called for the Unemployment Bill to be smashed "in its entirety." The following day there was a mass rally in Hyde Park, at which the speakers included Ellen Wilkinson and Dorothy Woodman, a writer and political activist. This time there was no violence from the police.

Some of the women and men who had marched to London went to the lobby of the House of Commons on 5 March to see their members of parliament. The prime minister refused to meet the marchers, though the women did get to meet his daughter, Miss Ishbel MacDonald, who told them that the training centres were "quite good." One woman responded tartly, "Why don't *you* go into domestic service and see how you like it?"

The agitation over the Means Test continued into the spring of 1935. In Manchester the Trades Council organised a march of the unemployed and employed on 5 March. There were two processions, one of which started from Ardwick Green, numbering about 800, and included a group of women who called themselves the "West Gorton Battalion of Lady Astor's Ragged Army" (Lady Astor was a Tory MP). The other, numbering about 150, started from Salford. The two processions converged on Whitworth Street West. In the course of the day the Trades Council submitted statements to the Mayors of Salford and Manchester, recalling a similar protest some three years before:

What, really, has been done for our unfortunate fellow citizens and their fellow citizens from then till now ? Unemployment, which moves across the working class like a plague, has claimed many additional victims. Though the figures of unemployment have been more or less static, the incidence of unemployment has changed. More homes have been wrecked. More families have been have been driven to the depths. More livelihoods have been shattered. More promising lives have been ruined.[6]

The 1936 Hunger March

In the autumn of 1936 another national march took place which again included a women's contingent. This was to be the largest Hunger March the NUWM ever organised, and the final one before the war. As in 1934 the movement actively canvassed support from the Labour Party and trade union movement. The TUC, however, still instructed Trades Councils not to support the march, although some did, defying the ban.

In Manchester, a Labour councillor, Wright Robinson, wrote a letter to the *Manchester Guardian* about the march:

On Wednesday October 21st between five hundred and six hundred Scottish hunger marchers, along with a number of Lancashire marchers, will arrive in Manchester on their way to London and will spend a night in our city. These men have been told officially that everything possible has been done for them, but they know that they still remain unemployed, with little prospect of employment, that they are easily forgotten, and that they are living in privation on meagre rations. They are taking this arduous method of reminding us of their existence and of our obligation.

Mrs Swenkie of Clydebank and Miss F Marsden of Bury on the 1934 march

An ad hoc committee has been set up to ensure that during their short stay in Manchester they have at least adequate food, clothing and shelter. Valuable help has already been given. More is needed. Golf clubs having men's serviceable footwear to give or friends able to make useful gifts should send them to All Saints Parish, York Street, Chorlton-on-Medlock, any day between 2pm and 5pm. Cash donations to the Marchers Reception fund should be sent or posted to me at the address given.[7]

The women's contingent started from Coventry on 28 October, heading south via Rugby, Daventry, Northampton, Newport Pagnell, Dunstable, St Albans, Finchley and Islington (where they were received by the Mayor). The traditional Hyde Park rally took place on 8 November.

On 4 November a letter was published in the *Manchester Guardian* signed by members of the Committee against Malnutrition, including such well-known figures such as the barrister D N Pritt and the writer and Labour councillor Edith Summerskill, in which they publicly challenged the BBC to put

Women marchers, 1936

STOP THIS STARVATION OF MOTHER and CHILD

By MAUD BROWN
(Women's Dept., N.U.W.M.)
PRICE ONE PENNY
Published by the National Unemployed Workers' Movement
11a, White Lion Street, London, E.1.

NUWM pamphlet by Maud Brown

Maud Brown & Mayor of Islington, 1936

the women marchers on the radio: **We understand that among the unemployed marchers now approaching London there is a contingent of women. It has long been our opinion that the working-class housewives are not only the first to suffer when the family income falls, but are at once the most maligned and least articulate members of our society. Very rarely have they the will or the opportunity to present their own case and we consider that the BBC will fulfil its duty to the public if it encourages two or three of these women to speak of their own lives in their own way and explain to the country why they have undertaken so arduous a march. We can do no less as a community for the women, who are or may be, the mothers of the coming generation.**[8]

Predictably the BBC did not take up this idea, so the Committee organised its own meeting in Essex Hall on The Strand on 10 November at which a number of the women spoke, describing in shocking detail their personal circumstances. One of them was Maggie Nelson, who told the audience that all three of her children had taken scholarships, and she had struggled to send them to the central school, yet now her two daughters were in domestic service while her son was working at a wage of 13 shillings a week. She herself was allowed 15 shillings a week to live on. The newspaper report continued:
Mrs. Nelson spoke of a baby in Blackburn which had died of pneumonia without a doctor and in a room without a fire, of another child which could not walk until it was five, and of the misery of watching children in Blackburn as they went to school. Running through her speech was the indignation of the working woman who had woven "miles of cloth," yet now had to do without towels and make sheets out of cheap scraps, the indignation of all Blackburn women whose pride it had once been that coal was brought to their doors, but now had to walk with bags to bring home four pennyworth of it.[9]

More stark facts about the suffering caused by unemployment and malnutrition were made plain at a public meeting in Manchester in the Memorial Hall, Albert Square, on 6 December 1936, called by the Manchester, Salford and District Maternal Mortality Committee. The chair was Alderman Wright Robinson, while the speakers included Dr Mabel May, of Didsbury, and two of the hunger marchers, Maggie Nelson and Mrs James of Accrington. It is worth quoting the newspaper report at length for the shocking accounts heard by the audience:
Dr. May, who had formerly served in the Maternity and Child Welfare Departments of Manchester and Rochdale Corporations, said that her own experience of the enormous number of people suffering from malnutrition in Manchester supported Sir John Orr's statement that there were four and a half million in the country with no more than 4s to 5s a week to spare for food. She ran her own household economically on one meal a day, yet it cost 15s to 18s per head per week for food. How much fresh fruit and vegetables could a family afford with only 4s to 5s per head per week for food? If the Minister of Health would only visit some of the Manchester and Salford clinics he would learn more than he appeared to know at present of the extent of malnutrition in the country.

Mrs. Nelson said a good deal had been said about unemployed persons going to "the pictures." It was true. In Blackburn there was a two-penny picture house and the unemployed went there when they could, to keep themselves sane. When she went on the "hunger march" she was "on the means test" because the mill in which she had been employed had had its machinery taken out and was now being used for making gas masks... In Oswaldtwistle there were now only three mills working out of fifteen, and the women were in a state of nervous breakdown.

While on the hunger march Mrs. Nelson asked thirty-two of the other women marchers how much milk they were able to get. The replies showed that there were only seven pints of fresh milk and 2s 4½d worth of tinned milk daily

for eighty persons. It was no use talking about the women of Lancashire not cooking their own food when they could not even afford to buy utensils to cook it in; nor was it of any use to ask why they did not make more use of the clinics when they had not clothing fit to be seen in there. The means test was breaking up the home life of the working people.

Mrs. James gave many other instances of hardship. One of her own children was unable to walk until four years of age because of lack of proper food. Many women in her district could afford neither the food to cook nor the coal to cook it with. She had had to push two children in a "pram" three miles twice a week to a clinic. One woman she met doing the same thing said: "I'm that hungry I cannot sleep." Another who could not give her child milk was told by a doctor to drink plenty of water in order to make more milk.[10]

Following the march the Manchester Reception Committee called a meeting in Caxton Hall on 19 December of trade unions, trades councils and Labour Party branches to discuss ways and means of rousing public opinion against the new UAB regulations and the Means Test, and to unite opinion in a demand for work schemes. The meeting passed a resolution expressing the belief that "the time was ripe for a united movement" on these issues.

After 1936 the NUWM declined from a mass movement to a pressure group. Richard Croucher suggests a number of reasons for this. Firstly, the numbers of unemployed began to fall in some areas, particularly in engineering, where there were more jobs as Britain began to re-arm as war seemed increasingly likely. Engineering had provided many of the NUWM activists. Secondly, the Communist Party, which provided many (though not all) of the NUWM activists was now turning its attention to other issue, particularly support for the Spanish Republic (where civil war had broken out in July 1936), and opposition to Oswald Mosley's British Union of Fascists. Wal Hannington wrote a history of the NUWM, *Unemployed Struggles 1919-1936*, which was published at the end of 1936, in effect drawing a line under its campaigning activity.

Forty years later Maud Brown wrote a short article for *Labour Monthly*, illustrated by a number of photographs from her archive:

When I look back on the old days and struggles, I realise that the conditions of life for working women have improved but little in my time. I was a member of the Edmonton Board of Guardians at a time when unemployment often meant separation of husband and wife in the workhouse, and the Relieving Officer would insist on the sale of any article of furniture before he gave an unemployed man a food voucher. In the twenties and thirties, hunger marches were aided by contingents of women from many parts led by such women as Emmie Lawther from Durham, Mrs Chater from Newcastle, Laura Johnson from Nottinghamshire and Fanny Deakin from Staffordshire. Harried by police and workhouse staff, these demonstrations had some hard-won success. They encouraged the fight against the means test and resisted Margaret Bondfield's efforts to force single women into domestic service... Those women who are young now must not fail to remember that what has been won has to be kept. During this International Women's Day Year, our old struggles should be kept constantly before all women.[11]

Fighting Fascism in Manchester

The British Union of Fascists (BUF) was founded by Sir Oswald Mosley in October 1932. Mosley came from an aristocratic family which had once owned much of Manchester, and was elected as Tory MP for Harrow in 1918. Clever, and an effective public speaker, a bright future seemed to beckon, but he left the party in protest at the actions of the Black and Tans in Ireland and eventually joined the Labour Party in 1924.

Mosley rose rapidly within the party and when Labour formed their second minority government in 1929, he was given a junior post as Chancellor of the Duchy of Lancaster. In 1930, as unemployment soared, he submitted a memorandum to the Cabinet advocating increased government spending in order to restart the economy, but this was rejected by the Chancellor, Philip Snowden, who stuck by the orthodox view that the government must reduce its spending to balance the books. Mosley resigned from the Labour Party in May 1930 and founded the New Party, attracting some support initially from the left of the Labour Party, such as John Strachey, MP.

The New Party put up a candidate, Allan Young, in a by-election in Ashton-under-Lyne in April 1931, attracting sufficient votes to take the seat from the Labour Party and hand it to the Tory Party. This led to Mosley being heckled by angry Labour supporters at the count, at which point, according to John Strachey, Mosley turned to him and remarked, "That is the crowd that has prevented anyone doing anything in England since the war." Strachey later wrote that it was at that moment that British Fascism was born.

Following a visit to Mussolini in Italy in January 1932 Mosley disbanded the New Party and set up the BUF. Its members were nick-named "Blackshirts" after the black shirts they customarily wore. Mosley and his lieutenants wore fascist-style military uniforms until these were banned in 1936.

The fascists built their movement through propaganda, public meetings and a large rally at Olympia in London in June 1934 at which anti-fascist hecklers were brutally beaten by BUF stewards. Mosley adopted an increasingly anti-semitic rhetoric in his speeches, and attempted to lead a mass BUF march through Jewish areas in the East End of London on 4 October 1936 with the protection of the police. However, there was a huge turnout by East Enders to oppose this and, after the police had failed to batter a path through the crowds (despite using mounted police wielding batons) the march was called off by the Chief Constable. The Battle of Cable Street, as it became known, did not mark the end of the BUF - whose activities continued up until 1940 - but it was the start of the movement's decline.

Evelyn Taylor and Jack Jones

Women Blackshirts

The British Union of Fascists' rally at Olympia on 7th June 1934

BUF activity wasn't just restricted to London. As a remedy for unemployment Mosley advocated the imposition of tariffs on foreign goods to protect British industry, and ran a strong campaign in Lancashire, where the cotton industry had been very badly hit by the Slump. Here too the BUF attracted fierce, and sometimes violent, opposition.

At one of his first meetings in Manchester, held in the Free Trade Hall on 12 March 1933 to launch their so-called "spring offensive" to build the BUF in industrial areas in the north, there was considerable trouble. BUF stewards attacked hecklers or those attempting to ask questions. At one point there was an outbreak of hand-to-hand fighting in the centre gangway, with BUF stewards apparently wielding rubber truncheons. The police eventually restored order, driving the stewards into the lobby.[12]

One of the leading women anti-fascists in Manchester was Evelyn Taylor, who was born in Knutsford in July 1913. She joined the Communist Party in the early 1930s, and was involved in the Mass Trespass by hundreds of ramblers on 24 June 1932 on Kinder Scout. Evelyn worked in a number of engineering factories in Manchester. She was fired from Ferguson and Pailins for union activity, but a strike by the National Society of Brass and Metal Mechanics won her reinstatement.

On 15 October 1933 Mosley spoke at a rally in Belle Vue, Manchester, marching out to a roll of drums and a blare of trumpets. Evelyn was in the audience and after a while stood up and started barracking him, whereupon Blackshirt stewards immediately attacked her. A comrade of hers, Benny Rothman, who was chucking leaflets into the audience, was also attacked by the fascists and thrown over the balcony, but luckily landed on some Blackshirts and was relatively unhamed.[13]

On 25 November 1934 the BUF held another meeting at the Free Trade Hall on the subjects of the trade depression in Lancashire and Indian Constutional Reform, with Mosley was the main speaker. In his speech he attacked Jews as an organised force in Britain who were "working up war feeling against countries like Germany," damaged British interests, and shown that they owed allegiance to others in foreign countries instead of Britain. "That would stop under Fascism," he promised. "We would stop alien immigration into this country, and what is more, send some people back to where they belong."

The hall was packed, and there were a number of disturbances by anti-fascists in the audience. Evelyn heckled Mosley several times from the gallery. Eventually he turned towards her and said, "I really must ask the Socialists not to send women to interrupt. If it must be done, let it be done by men," provoking cheering and booing in the audience. Mosley then went on to say that anyone who interrupted, and prevented the audience from hearing the speakers, would be removed "with the minimum of force," handed over to the police, and charged under the Public Meetings Act.

When Evelyn interrupted again, Mosley said that if any woman interrupted they would be put out by women. "We have women here, who will, if necessary put any Red woman out within two minutes." Several women Blackshirt stewards then grabbed Evelyn, and, after a fierce struggle lasting several minutes, she was carried out of the hall. Mosley told the audience, "I am sorry that you have had to witness such a scene, which was produced by the fact that the Socialist party in the utter cowardice of their generation have sent women to do their task. Any other woman who does the same thing will be charged as that lady will be charged. There is not an impartial man or woman in this hall who will not recognise that as a deliberate attempt to interfere with this meeting." There were further scuffles between stewards and anti-fascists at the back of the stalls: most of the protestors were ejected, some quite violently. After the meeting there were further scuffles outside the hall, and the police arrested ten people.[14]

At the instance of the fascists Evelyn and five men were summonsed under the Public Meetings Act for acting in a disorderly manner "for the purpose of preventing the transaction of the business for which the meeting was called." Mr W A Fearnley-Whittingstall, of Lewis and Co, London, appeared for the prosecution, while Mr Walter Wolfson appeared for the defence.

Fearnley-Whittingstall told the court that the defendants were among the people who had repeatedly interrupted Sir Oswald Mosley's speech, and that they had refused to desist when requested to do so by the stewards, some of whom, he alleged, were struck and kicked by the protestors. Richard Plathen, a BUF organiser, said there had been shouts of "Fascism Means Murder" and "Fascism Means War," and that there were struggles with the interrupters in the gallery.

Miss Marjorie Aitken told the court that she had warned Miss Taylor, but she had refused to be quiet and had seized a steward by the hair and spat at him. She had also been assaulted herself and had had to strike her in self-defence. Another steward, Cecily Weller, claimed that Evelyn had bitten her arm. In her defence Evelyn said that she had interjected three times during Mosley's speech, then someone had grabbed her arm and she had been struck and put out of the meeting. When she got to the bottom of the stairs, she had fainted. Evelyn denied having bitten Miss Weller.

Thomas Whittaker said he saw a woman Blackshirt put her arm behind Evelyn's neck and pull her head back, and saw another woman hit her in the face. When he protested at this, six Blackshirts had told him to shut up. At the end of the proceedings the stipendiary magistrate said he thought that Evelyn had been the worst offender. He fined her £3 for disrupting the meeting, and another £1 for the alleged assault on Miss Aitken.[15]

Evelyn appealed against the magistrate's decision, which was heard on 22 January 1935 by Sir Walter Greaves-Lord. Giving evidence at the appeal John Collins, who was in charge of the BUF stewards at the meeting, claimed that Evelyn had constantly interrupted Mosley and was warned to keep quiet. He left the women stewards to deal with her, as the male stewards were forbidden to touch women. Marjorie Aitken, who again gave evidence, claimed that she had heard Evelyn shout something about "Dirty Mosley" among other things. "I told her that if she could not keep quiet she must go out. There was a light scuffle between a steward and a man next to Miss Taylor. She then struck the steward so I thought it was time I stepped in." She also claimed that Evelyn made "a fiendish attack" on her, tearing her blouse and skirt, kicking her, and pulling her hair.

Evelyn strongly contested this version of events. She said she was struck by Miss Aitken first and hit her back. She was then seized from behind and almost choked. It was then that she kicked, and afterwards fainted. She admitted interrupting Mosley three times, but denied some of the remarks attributed to her. Evelyn maintained that she had gone to the Free Trade Hall to expose fascism by questions. But her appeal was dismissed.[16]

In early 1936 Evelyn went to Moscow to work for Abramoff (Jacob Miron), the deputy head of the Finance Department at the Comintern, and was used to convey messages and money to the underground Communist Parties and anti-fascist organisations in Germany, Hungary, Czechoslovakia and Italy.

Returning to England, Evelyn started a relationship with George Brown, a leading member of the Communist Party in Manchester: the couple got married in January 1937 on the eve of his departure for Spain to act as Political Commissar for the International Brigade. She never saw him again as he was killed at Brunete on 7 July 1937. In 1938 Evelyn married Jack Jones, a trade unionist and Labour councillor who had also fought in Spain. During the Second World War they lived in Coventry, where Evelyn worked on a production line and was a shop steward. In the 1950s Evelyn joined the Labour Party, and was also active in CND. In 1968 Jack became General Secretary of the Transport and General Workers' Union. Evelyn died in 1999.[17]

Fighting Fascism in Spain

The Spanish Civil War started on 17 July 1936 when sections of the army attempted to overthrow the government

Lillian Urmston (right) in Spain

Fighting in the Spanish Civil War

Molly Murphy in Spain

of the Republic. It was the culmination of years of bitter political division. In 1930 a Republic was proclaimed after the king, Alphonso XIII, abdicated. Republicans and socialists won the elections that followed, embarking on a programme of modest social reforms which was bitterly resisted by the Roman Catholic church, landowners and sections of the army.

In 1933 a right-wing government came to power and reversed the reforms. But in February 1936 a Popular Front government of republicans, socialists and communists won the elections and instigated another programme of reforms. In response a number of generals, including Francisco Franco, began preparations for an army coup. They rose first in Morocco, using it as a base for sending troops across to Spain, assisted by Germany. On the Spanish mainland self-organised workers' militias fought the coup in many cities, and initially only the major city of Seville fell to the Nationalists as the rebels called themselves. Spain was divided: civil war followed.

The Republican government held about two thirds of the country to begin with, but was poorly armed. France and Britain did nothing to aid the Republic, instead supporting a "Non-Intervention" policy which banned arms sales. Hitler and Mussolini signed up to the policy, but then blatantly ignored it, sending arms, aircraft and soldiers to the rebels.

An international movement of volunteers – the International Brigades - numbering around 40,000 came to the aid of the beleaguered Republic. This included around 2,500 men and women from Britain and Ireland, many of whom were wounded, while over 400 killed. In addition to those who went to fight, thousands of people were involved in solidarity committees, raising money and sending food and medical aid. The cause of Spain became a rallying cry for many on the left, who feared that fascism was marching across Europe unchallenged, and must be stopped at all costs. For some it was a cause to which they devoted the rest of their lives.

Women went to Spain as journalists, photographers, ambulance drivers and nurses. Some were members of left parties who had a political commitment to defending the Republic and halting the advance of fascism in Europe, others went for humanitarian reasons, shocked by the bombing of civilians by the Nationalist airforce. The nurses included two women from the Manchester area: Molly Murphy and Lillian Urmston.

Molly Murphy (née Morris)

Molly was born in Leyland in 1890. In 1900 the family was forced to move to the slums of Salford after her father resigned from his job as a factory manager in support of the workers in his department when their wage claim was rejected. "That sounds very fine and noble," she later wrote, "but coming from a man with a family of six to provide for, it was just plain silly."

Molly joined the Women's Social and Political Union (the suffragettes) when she was 16, along with her mother. In 1912, aged 22, she became an organiser for the WSPU in Sheffield. Under the direction of Christabel Pankhurst the movement was now using arson as a tactic to put pressure on the Liberal government to concede Votes for Women. Molly, and a number of other women, regularly set fire to postboxes in Sheffield, using incendiary devices supplied to them from their sisters in London.

For Molly the fight for votes for women was a part of "a very positive phase of the human struggle for socialism and not something apart from it." After leaving the WSPU she trained as a nurse in Hammersmith and married Jack Murphy, whom she had met in Sheffield. They both joined the Communist Party in its early years, and went on a trip to Moscow where they met Lenin. In the early 1930s they left the Communist Party and joined the Labour Party.

Molly says that, when she heard about the appeal for nurses to go to Spain, it "rang a bell in my heart." She thought it would be "nauseating" to carry on as a private nurse "when splendid young men were dying on the international battlefield of Spain because there were so few nurses and doctors to help them to keep alive." To begin with she was turned down, but then in January 1937 Molly received a telegram asking if she was still available. "When I received the telegram calling me, it seemed like a ray of light amidst the greyness of the day."

On the train going to Albacete, the headquarters of the International Brigade, Molly and the other nurses were presented with oranges, grapes and dates by the Spanish people at every station where the train stopped. From Albacete she was posted to a hospital near the Madrid front:

When we arrived in the early hours of the morning in the deepest darkness it all seemed so weird and grim. Fighting had been hard and fierce in recent days. The hospital was crowded to capacity. Every bed was occupied and wounded men lay on mattresses covering every foot of space. All was dark and the nurse was moving about the place with the aid of a shaded torch. The black-out had to be very complete.[18]

Molly soon discovered that working conditions for the nurses in Spain were very different from those that she had been used to in Britain:

Regulation hours of work meant all hours. Never did we get a house for conversion where there was a laid-on supply of water. Always the water had to be carried, rarely less than a quarter of a mile. There were no windows. All had been shattered by blast from bombs. One had to get used to the breezes blowing through the place, to rats scurrying across our beds, to bats flying around in the night, to living with wounded men groaning with pain, to working until one was completely exhausted, to fall asleep on a blood soaked mattress and to wake up with a start finding wounded men on either side.[19]

The medical staff were so over-worked that they often had little idea of what was happening outside of the hospital in which they were placed:

It was not possible for us to follow the fortunes of the war as a whole. Indeed, sometimes we had not the slightest notion of where we were in relation to

the general line of the war, and we were so engrossed in the work that was thrust upon us by the war in our immediate area that we learned our location on the map later on. [20]

According to Molly, they used their occasional leisure time between battles for "having a wash and brush up" and "letting our people at home know we were still in the land of the living and reading our letters." For her birthday the theatre staff gave Molly a present of enough hot water to wash her feet and "promised for my next birthday to give some more for the rest of my body!!!" The women often suffered from lice, as well as dysentery (or its opposite). Molly wrote home that "the sanitary arrangements are such that chronic constipation is a gift from the Gods."

After her return to England Molly struggled to adjust to peace and to being with her family again:
It was splendid to be once more with my loved ones, and yet I was not happy. Time and again for hours I was living again with those I had left behind on the fluctuating front of the war in Spain. So many were dead who had been near to me… And I lived over and over again the dark nights when we picked our way between the beds and the mattresses on the floor, with covered flashlights and the bombs fell nearby and men groaned in pain. I saw again the girl in the street of Madrid with her face shot off and the corpses laid on the side of the street after a raid or heavy gunfire, waiting to be taken away. I was sinking into a nervous depression as the tiredness got the upper hand.[21]

During the Second World War Molly worked as a nurse with a mobile medical unit in London dealing with victims of the Blitz, until she had a nervous breakdown. In time she recovered, but she never returned to nursing.

When Molly wrote her autobiography she called it *Nurse Molly,* for her identity as a nurse was very important to her. However when it was finally published after her death, edited by Ralph Darlington, it was called *Molly Murphy: Suffragette and Socialist.*

Lillian Buckoke (née Urmston)

Lillian was born in 1915, and grew up in the Cheshire mill town of Stalybridge. Her mother had gipsy ancestry, and Lillian would apparently wander off with gypsies as a little girl. Her father claimed to be descended from the rebel leader, Jack Cade, and would tell her about him, "The more I've read about him since, the more proud I am that in a small way perhaps I've tried to carry on his tradition," she later said.

Stalybridge, like many northern textile towns, was badly hit by the Slump: Lillian recalled crossing the road to avoid meeting people she knew who were queuing outside the Labour Exchange:
They were standing there looking hungry, depressed and ashamed, and I used to feel ashamed that I'd even glanced at them because I felt it was adding to their misery. And then I heard stories of the way they were treated, when the money was pushed across the counter it was often pushed so that coins fell onto the floor, when the man had to touch his cap and pick them up they were told, "Hurry up, hurry up, there's a long queue behind you, you know, get out of the way."[22]

Lillian qualified as a nurse and joined the Territorial Army Nursing Service. She was not a member of the Labour Party or Communist Party, but her sympathies, she later reflected, were always with the "underdog." Lillian was working as a Staff Nurse in a nursing home in the Lake District when she saw an appeal for medical volunteers in the *News Chronicle,* which prompted her to apply to Spanish Medical Aid to go to Spain, but was bitterly disappointed to receive no reply, despite contacting them numerous times. Finally, in frustration, Lillian sent them a telegram asking why they had not replied. This worked, and in early 1937 she was seen by the secretary, George Jeger. He asked her many questions, including why she had written "politically disinterested" on her form. "Well, I've never heard of any organisation employing nurses that wanted nurses who were politically minded," Lillian replied.

After being accepted Lillian handed in her notice which did not go down well with her employers:
I was requested to be ready to go at anytime and they would send phials through the post of anti-typhoid – anti-typhus serum and so on for me to take. So I gave in my notice immediately and I had about three weeks leave due and the sisters who ran the nursing home refused to give me the leave. They refused to pay me my uniform allowance which was overdue and they threatened me with all sorts of dire things, including a solicitor's letter if I left them. They also confiscated from my bedroom the phials of serum which I had to have.[23]

Lillian was helped by a doctor working in the home, who happened to be a Quaker, and gave her the necessary injections, while Spanish Medical Aid gave the sum of £5 which her employers had insisted she must pay for leaving early.

In June 1937 Lillian journeyed to Spain along with an Australian nurse, Dorothy Low. When they arrived in Portbou, just across the Spanish border in Catalonia, there was nobody to meet them, and, even though they had passports and visas, the two women ended up being detained and locked up in a hotel room. They were taken out to eat under guard, and fortunately came across the two men who had been sent to meet them. After this initial bad experience things got much better for Lillian and Dorothy, and on the rest of their journey they were warmly greeted by ordinary Spaniards.

Lillian nursed on the Aragon front, in Teruel, and in a railway tunnel near Flix. In the course of her work she formed a number of close friendships with Spanish women, in particular Lola, who had been a "miliciana," one of the civilian women who took up arms in the first weeks of the war to fight the Nationalist coup, but were then disarmed by the Republican army. Lola's parents had been killed in Andalucia. Molly recalled:
She was a tiny little thing, Lola, and everybody worshipped her – she was always bright and gay and it was only when she slept at night you realised all the tension that was building up in her.

Manchester solidarity rally for Spain

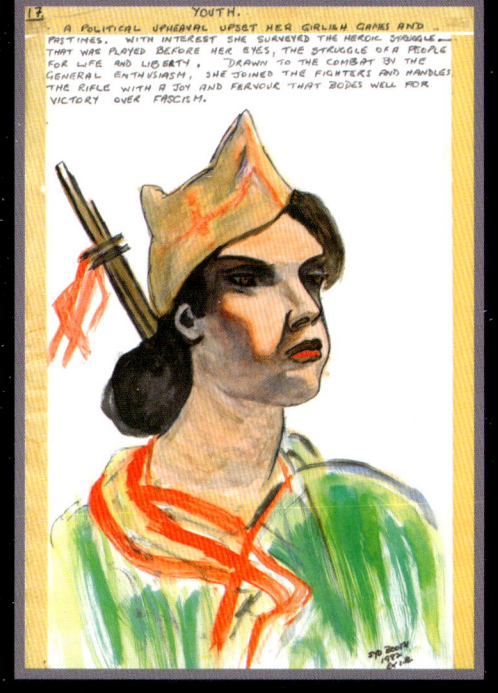

Watercolours by Syd Booth

She used to have terrible nightmares, and when we slept out in the open, we were near to Nationalist lines, we always had to be ready to clap a hand over her mouth when she wakened because she was babbling and screaming with the horror of what had happened in her Andalucian town.[24]

After the defeat of the Republic in March 1939 Lillian crossed the border to France where she was held in a refugee camp until her colleague Rosita Dawson arranged for her release. During the Second World War Lillian was an army nursing officer, and was badly wounded by shell fire at Anzio, Italy, leaving her with spinal injuries from which she never fully recovered. After the war she worked as journalist for a number of newspapers.

Lillian, now married, returned to Spain in 1949, 1953 and 1964, visiting the parts of the country where she had nursed:
My husband was greatly impressed, that, on these three trips, someone always recognised me, called out "Lilliana" and brought out groups of those who had known me. Invariably, we ate, drank and reminisced, despite the interest shown by the Guardia Civil. As I'd become a writer/journalist, I was able to take money to help some of those in need.[25]

Lillian died in October 1990. Some years later a blue plaque in her memory was placed at St Paul's Primary School, Huddersfield Road, Stalybridge, where she had been a pupil.

Elsie Booth's story

Back home in Britain women had to cope when their men went to Spain to fight, often having to brave suspicion and hostility from their neighbours, as well as struggling to make ends meet. In Manchester one such woman was Elsie Booth.

Elsie was born in 1914, the youngest child in a working class family. After her father died when she was 15, her mother scrubbed floors and was a regular customer at the pawn shop, taking in clothes in an effort to make ends meet. She died a year later. As Elsie reflected, "what killed her really was the bloody worry of living."

Elsie worked in a cotton mill where she joined the trade union and then became interested in politics. She joined the Friends of the Soviet Union, and then the Communist Party, which offered young people both educational and social activities with classes on politics and economics, meetings and rallies, as well as camps and rambles in the countryside. It was a new world for her. "I only really started living when I joined the Communist Party, before that life was nothing really." In 1932, aged 18, she married a fellow Communist, Syd Booth.

She attempted to persuade the women she worked with to take an interest in politics, but with little success:
The mill girls used to think I was mad when I took an interest in politics because they'd never heard of it you see. They used to go to a dance or stand at the corner talking to boys, that was their life. And when they knew that I'd joined the Communist Party, well, they all expected me to pull a bomb out from under my coat.[26]

Elsie was active in the Workers' Birth Control Group and the Maternal Mortality Group. In 1934 she was one of 70 delegates from Britain who went to Paris for the first international congress of Women Against War and Fascism. Politics was very important to her, and she did her best to keep on attending Communist Party meetings, even after she had children:
You had to come home and see to your kids, and then you had to go and bring one out of the nursery and - no washing machines – you had to go to the public wash house with an old trolley and bring it back. I had to leave my son in the house minding the baby... so you sort of had to put an extra spurt on and try and assert yourself, which was very hard to do. This is the reason why it was always a struggle to get women in the Party in the thirties, because - I don't care what anybody says – the men domineered the women, especially in the working-class areas. The ordinary working women didn't really have much of a chance unless you really did assert yourself – you couldn't walk out and

leave the kids, somebody had to mind them, didn't they?[27]

Syd wanted to go to Spain, and, despite her personal misgivings, Elsie felt that she had to agree:

..., he kept asking me, "I want to go to Spain," and you've got a baby eighteen months old, and although I was a member of the Communist party myself – I read the Daily Worker, I knew all about it, and I went to the meetings - but you don't want your own to go, do you? And I knew he should go, but he wouldn't go until I said "Yes," you see, but of course, he was always maundering me. So eventually, I gave in at the end.[28]

Elsie had to go down to the Communist Party offices to confirm her agreement, which she did with Syd having been sent out of the room. The party official questioned her, asking "he's not pushing you, is he? "Oh no, no," replied Elsie, " I want him to go." Syd left a week later: The night he was going, I went to the station, he didn't want me to go but I went... I couldn't feel myself walking... As that train went - it was a terrible feeling... And you couldn't tell anybody, you see, you lived in a little street and you couldn't tell the neighbours, and of course, after a few weeks all the neighbours thought he'd deserted you, you know – they didn't understand. Then you had your family saying, "What has he left you for? Has he deserted you?" So you had all this to deal with. Very hard it was. [29]

Whilst Syd was away, Elsie was unable to find work as she had a child to look after. She had to rely on support from her comrades in the party (who invited her round for meals), and on 30 shillings a week from the Dependants Aid Committee, formed in June 1937. Sometimes she didn't have enough money to pay the rent and had to pawn her wedding ring. Syd was wounded in Spain, and Elsie was even told that he was dead, but he made it home in the end. Elsie summed up her experience, "... I always say, them that was left behind suffered just as much."

When the Second World War started, Elsie got a job as a shop assistant in a Co-operative store, and later worked in a Corporation Electric Works. In 1941 she had another child, a girl. Elsie remained active in the Communist Party for many years. She died in 1996.

Notes

[1] Noreen Branson and Margot Heinemann, Britain in the Nineteen Thirties (1971), p. 5.

[2] Sue Bruley, Leninism, Stalinism and the Women's Movement Between the Wars 1920-1939 (2012), p. 46.

[3] National Archives www.nationalarchives.gov.uk/education/topics/marchers.htm

[4] Maud Brown, Stop this Starvation of Mother and Child (1935), pp. 6-7.

[5] Maud Brown, Stop This Starvation of Mother and Child (1935), p. 13.

[6] Manchester Guardian, 5 March 1935, p. 20.

[7] Manchester Guardian, 17 October 1936, p. 15

[8] Manchester Guardian, 4 November 1936, p. 20.

[9] Manchester Guardian, 11 November 1936, p. 14

[10] Manchester Guardian, 7 December 1936, p. 11.

[11] Labour Monthly, March 1975. According to an article on the internet Maud died on 29 June 1975, aged 86.

[12] Manchester Guardian, 13 March 1933, p. 9.

[13] Dave Hann, Physical Resistance, A Hundred Years of Anti-Fascism, (2013), p. 31.

[14] Manchester Guardian, 26 November 1934, p. 9 and p. 11.

[15] Manchester Guardian, 6 December 1934, p. 11.

[16] Manchester Guardian, 23 January 1935, p. 5.

[17] Obituary in Manchester Guardian, 5 January 1999, p. 18.

[18] Angela Jackson, British Women and the Spanish Civil War (2009), p. 139.

[19] Angela Jackson, British Women and the Spanish Civil War (2009), p. 140.

[20] Angela Jackson, British Women and the Spanish Civil War (2009), p. 150.

[21] Angela Jackson, British Women and the Spanish Civil War (2009), p. 246.

[22] Angela Jackson, British Women and the Spanish Civil War (2009), p. 50.

[23] Angela Jackson, British Women and the Spanish Civil War (2009), p. 127.

[24] Angela Jackson, British Women and the Spanish Civil War (2009), p. 160.

[25] Angela Jackson, British Women and the Spanish Civil War (2009), p. 267.

[26] Angela Jackson, British Women and the Spanish Civil War (2009), p. 53.

[27] Angela Jackson, British Women and the Spanish Civil War (2009), p. 86.

[28] Angela Jackson, British Women and the Spanish Civil War (2009), p. 111.

[29] Angela Jackson, British Women and the Spanish Civil War (2009), p. 112.

Women and the Second World War

"Get the women organised, and then we can end the war this year."

Unlike August 1914, Britain's declaration of war on Germany on 3 September 1939, was greeted, not with celebrating crowds in the streets, but with grim determination as something desperately unwanted - but in the end unavoidable. For those who had campaigned in the scant twenty years between the two wars for a new international order to avoid war and guarantee peace, it was simply heartbreaking.

Evacuation

Even before the war began many Manchester women experienced the deep emotional trauma of sending their children away for their safety. It was firmly believed by the government's military experts that at the outbreak of war there would be immediate mass bombing of British cities by the Luftwaffe, resulting in huge casualties. It was also expected that poison gas would be used, and so everybody in the country, including children and babies, was issued with a gas mask to be carried at all times.

When it became clear over the summer of 1939 that war was just weeks away, the government completed its plans for the mass evacuation of three million children and mothers the moment that war was declared. Nothing on this scale had ever been attempted before in the history of the country.

The Ministry of Health divided the country into three areas: neutral, evacuation, and reception. In July 1939 the government sent out a leaflet, *Evacuation: Why and How*, to every household in the country, setting out the areas from which people would be evacuated if they wished. It emphasised that the scheme was entirely a voluntary one but added "clearly the children will be much safer and happier away from the big cities where the dangers will be greatest."

The list of areas to be evacuated included Manchester, where a total of 71,000 school children, 58,000 pre-school children and 4,000 expectant mothers had been registered, representing 71 % of the school population and 18% of the population of the city.

The Ministry made a broadcast on 24 August, asking teachers in the evacuation areas to return to their schools. Parents were told to provide each child with a gas mask, a change of underclothes, house shoes or plimsolls, spare stockings or socks, toothbrush and comb, a towel and handkerchiefs, a warm coat or mackintosh and a bag of food to last the day.

Still hoping that war could be averted at the last minute the government hesitated for several days before finally issuing an instruction on 31 August for the evacuation to begin the next day. In Manchester the *Manchester Guardian* reporter went to the Old Moat elementary school to observe how things went:

Sometimes parents or older children were with them, but they were mostly alone. One did not see a child who was not tidily fitted for the journey and what lies ahead – a little trim, perhaps, rather as though they had brought rucksacks to Sunday school. As the children assembled they went to their usual class-rooms, where the registers were marked, labels issued and affixed, rucksacks inspected, groups formed and leaders appointed - and well before nine o'clock the children were marshalled in the yard and fifteen buses were waiting.

Some mothers and fathers, several milkmen, babies in prams, several dogs... had collected in the roadway... The children were in perfect control, as cheerful as they were orderly. There was no singing or shouting but an eager occupation of the buses, and all the usual competition to get a seat "on the top" or at the window, and there was eagerness among those in the crowd to locate their own child.

"There she is on top," one excited mother cried, seizing a neighbour's arm. "Can you see our Noreen? Ta-ta luv. Be a good girl." There was no goodbye. It was always "Ta-ta," with occasional last instructions...

Between six and seven hundred children with helpers had been accommodated in a dozen buses in twenty minutes and they had moved off to Belle Vue station. It was an absolutely well-ordered and characteristically undemonstrative departure, carried out to time and with a good heart. And when the buses had all

page 43

gone one mother asked another, "They'll be all right won't they? " "Of course they will," was the emphatic reply.[1]

By the evening a total of 268 Manchester schools had been closed down, while an astonishing total of 46,276 children and 2,000 teachers had been evacuated. Amongst the Manchester children sent off was Peter Heaton, who recalled many years later:

In the early hours of Friday morning 1st September, aged five I was taken to school with my brother and two sisters. No doubt registers were called and a large group made their way to the local railway station named Belle Vue in Gorton, Manchester. As the children boarded the steam train, heading to a secret safe destination away from Manchester, which we were told was going to be a very dangerous place with bombing etc., much advice was shouted to the children - such as "Stick together.","Look after your brother." "Look after your sister." "Remember to write."

We towny child evacuees wore labels and were provided with sufficient food for 24 hours carried in a haversack, a carrier bag or a pillow case. The food included a tin of corned beef, a tin of condensed milk, biscuits, fruit; in addition we had a change of clothing and our gas mask.

We... travelled 15 miles from Manchester to Poynton, Cheshire. We congregated in a school hall for the "choosing", which turned out to be a most traumatic time awaiting selection by the local residents. Needless to say fair-haired pretty girls and robust boys aged 12-14 were the most sought-after.

My brother Robert and I were selected to stay with a middle-aged childless couple. We only stayed there one week, then moved on. I personally stayed a total of three years at a total of three homes.[2]

The Manchester evacuees were sent to villages and towns in Cheshire, Lancashire and Cumbria, with some of the lucky ones ending up at the seaside on the Fylde coast. The *Manchester Guardian* reported:

The holiday-makers welcomed them enthusiastically and normally shy children soon grew accustomed to giving a full account of themselves to people who stopped them in the streets. The main burden of keeping children in order during the day falls on the teacher, but early on Saturday morning quite a number of children were to be seen walking with their new "mothers" helping to carry home the morning shopping.

One woman who had lost both her own children when young had taken in two girls from Hulme and announced her intention of "rigging them out" with new clothes, keeping them in pocket-money, and, in general, treating them as her own family. Some of the evacuees were sent to houses where there were already visitors staying... On Saturday evening, before bedtime some of these visitors were to be seen shepherding their new young friends around, giving them pennies to put in slot machines, and explaining to passers-by, "They're from Manchester. We're just giving them a bit of a treat." [3]

The evacuation itself had gone very smoothly, but what the authorities had not allowed for (although it could perhaps have been anticipated, given the unprecedented distress for parents and disruption of family life created by the evacuation) was that once it was over, and with no bombing raids on Manchester having occurred as predicted, many parents quickly reconsidered their decision and brought their children back home.

The reasons given by mothers for returning included, "...homesickness, nervous agitation, difficulty in establishing relations with billeting householders (in some instances arising from acute consciousness of class differences), a feeling of strangeness in rural surroundings felt by some people of urban habit ..." [4]

On the first weekend after the evacuation a considerable number of parents either took their own cars or hired vehicles to bring back children, while others brought their children back by train or coach. Manchester Council's Education

Burning building in Manchester, December 1940

Manchester evacuees leaving their school

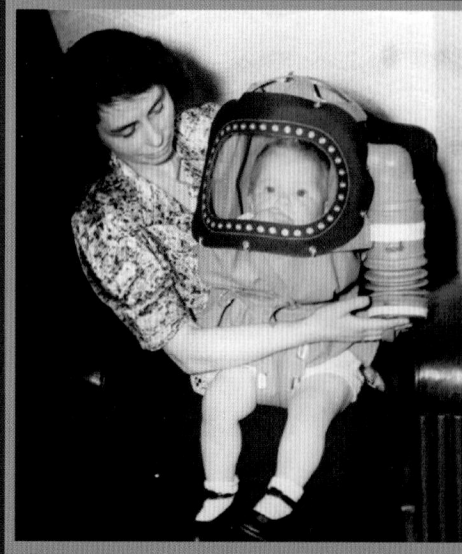

Child in a gas mask

Manchester evacuees going from the buses to the train station

Air-raid shelter on Hyde Road, Manchester

Manchester firefighters putting out a blaze after a bombing raid

Department estimated that by the end of September 13,963 children had returned home, with another 11,969 children coming back in October. The numbers returning home were particularly high for mothers and pre-school children, of whom 16,969 returned out of 29,901.[5]

In November the Council issued a report on the evacuation, in which it noted that problems had begun on the second day, with some women unable to adjust to being out in the country and away from friends and neighbours. There were also problems with how some women were treated, quoting one case of a mother "who had left her own good home to put her children in safety" being made to eat her meals from the draining board of the kitchen sink. The report summed up what it described as "the human aspects" of the evacuation:

It was clear... that often householders in the reception areas have been set a task quite beyond their physical and social resources. There were some... wholly unable to adjust themselves to the responsibilities of billeting children; some were invalids; some had always lived rather solitary lives; many who could be happy with the children could not tolerate the parent... There were also many difficulties created by parents who visited householders and altogether failed to appreciate their points of view. Often there was dissatisfaction on both sides, resulting in acrimonious arguments, in appeals to the tribunals, and in withdrawals.[6]

Faced with thousands of children roaming the city who were not in school, the Education Committee agreed on 18 December to re-open six secondary schools and enough elementary schools to provide at least one in every ward. By the following spring 11,000 children were attending full time classes, 10,000 were in part-time classes and a further 16,000 were attending tutorial classes at another 130 schools. The Department also opened up 18 centres to provide free school meals every day to 1,800 children as well as free school milk.

The Luftwaffe began bombing London and other cities in September 1940, and the long feared bombing of Manchester took place on the nights of 22/23 and 23/24 December when German aircraft dropped tons of high explosives and incendiaries, killing at least 684 people, and setting fire to many buildings in the city centre.

In the wake of the air-raids the Education Department carried out a completely fresh registration on 28 December, believing that parents may have changed their outlook. It opened up all schools in Manchester to do so, except those in Wythenshawe, which was still deemed a "neutral area." Those parents who had registered earlier in the year had to register afresh. There was a sluggish response, leading to Ministry of Information loud-speakers being sent out to tour the city, reminding parents that children could still be registered.

On 2 January and 3 January 1941 9,581 children "warmly clad, securely labelled and equipped with gas masks, lunch-bags and a change of clothes apiece" (according one press report) were evacuated, many of them veterans of the first evacuation. Most of them were from the schools in the poorer districts, and the more heavily bombed central districts of the city. They joined some 5,000 other children who still remained outside Manchester from the original evacuation.

Manchester was bombed again several times in 1941, but not on the same scale as the Christmas Blitz, and, as the danger from the air lessened, many parents brought their children home again. Ironically, in August 1944 hundreds of women and children were evacuated to Manchester from the south of England, which was being hit every day by the German's new weapon, the V1 "Flying Bomb." The Lord Mayor Alderman Leonard Cox said:

The evacuees who are coming to stay with us have been driven from their homes by the use of a ruthless and inhuman weapon. Their stay is purely temporary and its length will not be determined by the enemy but by the strength of the arms of the United Nations... In the meantime I am sure we shall be pleased to give them a place in our homes.[7]

Some children evacuated from Manchester stayed away for the duration of the war. In their annual report, issued in March 1945, by the Wood Street Mission (which was used as a distribution centre for returning children) the Secretary, Major F W Towns, explained that "there were parents who did not know and had to be introduced by the officers to their own children, who had left them in the early days of the war."

Women War Workers

The government introduced conscription for all men aged between 18 and 41 on the day that war was declared. Although women were not initially conscripted, many did come forward to volunteer in the first months of the war. Two companies of the Women's Auxiliary Air Force were established in Manchester in September 1939, for instance. Women in the armed forces did not fight, however, but were confined to administrative and clerical jobs or working as drivers. A small number of women did get to work on anti-aircraft batteries, although Winston Churchill expressly prevented them from actually firing the guns! Other women served in the early warning radar stations.

A number of women MPs from both parties, such as Edith Summerskill (Labour) and Irene Ward (Conservative), established a Woman Power Committee in May 1940, which pressurised the Ministry of Labour for more action on recruiting women. One of the members of the Committee, Mary Sutherland, said in September 1941:

I am convinced that if the married women are to be mobilised effectively for the war effort, the question of organising work to meet the circumstances of the married woman needs to be considered much more thoroughly than has hitherto been the case. Married women who are considered available just cannot be fitted into an industrial organisation which is planned primarily to receive workers who have no other occupation.[8]

Ernest Bevin was against compulsion to begin with, believing that women would work harder if they were volunteers. However, in March 1941 the government

Women factory workers

asked all women aged 19-40, whether they were at work or not, to register with the Employment Exchange.

As well as central government directives, there were also local initiatives. In September 1941 the authorities staged a fortnight-long recruiting campaign in Manchester to encourage women to take up war-work, which included staging an exhibition in Lewis's department store, stationing a recruiting van in the city centre in Piccadilly, and dispatching women in loud-speaker vans to tour local areas. On 13 September women munition-workers and women in the services paraded together from Ardwick to the city centre, where the Lord Mayor took the salute in Albert Square. The campaign was a success: over 4,000 women made enquiries regarding war-work, resulting in 510 women joining the various women's services, whilst 481 transferred to work on munitions.

In December 1941 the government bit the bullet and introduced conscription for women, although, at Bevin's insistence, women were still given the choice between joining the services, working in civil defence or working in munition factories. Married women were exempted, but the call-up of single women or childless widows aged 20 to 30 began in January 1942. As well as the armed forces, 80,000 women joined the Land Army, working on farms as they had during the First World War. A number of other women worked in forestry or on the canals.

Edith Summerskill believed that the changes being brought about by the war would alter women's lives for the better:

Poster encouraging women to go into engineering

Article in *Home Front* magazine, July 1944

Fears have been expressed that communal feeding and crèches herald the disintegration of family life after the war. Some of the worst features of home life are certainly threatened, to the dismay of the domestic Hitlers who revel in the petty dictatorships which they have established. The freedom which women are enjoying today will spell the doom of home life as enjoyed by the male who is lord and master immediately he enters his own front door. I hope that communal feeding has convinced us of the stupid waste of fuel, food and labour entailed in millions of families each day cooking their meals on millions of separate gas stoves. It must at least have shown the housewife that she is not indispensable, and that on occasions the family can feed well and cheaply, while she takes a day off to spend as she thinks fit. There is a curious belief which is shared by most men that women instinctively love cooking and washing up. A perfectly cooked meal is certainly an achievement and a woman may well experience pleasure in producing a savoury and appetising dish. But I have never known ecstasy induced by washing up.[9]

During the war the number of women in work rose to an estimated 7,500,000 out of a total workforce of 22,285,000. The war also changed the gender structure of many industries - for its duration at least - as many industries, where women had been in a small minority before the war, saw their numbers rise two or threefold. By 1945 women made up 60% of the workforce in electrical engineering, 52% in chemicals, 46% in metals and 34% in engineering. Caroline Haslett, Secretary of the Women's Engineering Society, asserted in 1941 that "it was the job that mattered and not the sex of the worker." Official government propaganda films and posters emphasised the role that women workers were playing in the war.

Part-time Work

Despite the best efforts of the government, many women were reluctant to enter full-time work because they were responsible for looking after husbands and children at home. This began to change as firms started to offer more part-time work in a bid to attract women, leading to the numbers of women working part-time increasing as the war went on.

In June 1942, for instance, the *Manchester Guardian* reported that it was firms not directly concerned with war work which were taking on part-time staff as they released their full-time workers to the armed forces or munitions factories. These included a major laundry, a large department store, the Post Office (where women sorted and delivered the letters), and a municipal gas department where women were sent out to collect the money from slot-meters. The report noted that for this work "the women wear a uniform with trouser: this is hard work and would be specially hard on stockings." In a Post Office in "a northern town" women were now working an 18-hour week from 7am to 10am, preparing their letters for their "walk," and then doing the delivery. A number of women also did a few hours work in the evening, collecting the mail, helping to sort it out, and assisting in the dispatch.[10]

As the labour shortage in industry worsened, the government forced reluctant employers to recruit part-time staff. By the end of 1943 there were 700,000 part-time women workers, which rose to 900,00 by the end of 1944.

Some women found part-time work liberating. Mass-Observation recorded the views of a 40-year-old housewife:

I thoroughly enjoy my four hours working here in the afternoon. I'm all agog to get here. After all, for a housewife who's been a cabbage for fifteen years - you feel you've got out of the cage and you're free. Quite a lot of the part-timers feel like that - to get out and see some new faces - it's all so different, such a change from dusting. I think the war has made a lot of differences to housewives. I don't think they'll want to go back to the old narrow life.[11]

Welfare for Women War Workers in Manchester

Single women could be directed to wherever they were needed - even if it was a long way from home - which meant

page 47

they had to live in digs or hostels. On 22 October 1942 the Lord Mayor of Manchester, Alderman Wright Robinson, officially opened the Hartley Hall hostel in Whalley Range for women war workers, set up by the Young Women's Christian Association. The hostel had accommodation for 106 munition-workers in 53 double-bedrooms, and for 93 other war workers in single-rooms.

Mr Vincent, welfare officer to the Ministry of Labour in the north-west, said that the government has "the very unpleasant duty" of bringing a very large number of young people away from their homes:

Many had never lived in a great city or worked in a large factory before. Many had been "directed" and even the journey was a terrifying experience. Comfortable accommodation on arrival was of the utmost importance. There was also a very practical side of the problem. It did not require much knowledge of psychology to know that mental unhappiness was reflected in physical condition and consequently in such things as absenteeism. The number of genuine cases of indigestion which occurred among women was amazing, and he was something of a psychologist who first used the word "homesickness" because there was a connection between homesickness and physical illness. For that reason alone what the YWCA was doing at Hartley Hall was of immense value.[12]

In October 1942 a Recreation Club for women war workers was opened in Urmston by the North–West War-Workers' Clubs' Committee, whose Secretary was Miss H Johnson. The following year they opened three more in Sale, Eccles and Stretford. The Committee worked with the Ministry of Labour on the social and recreational side of dealing with the problems of transferred workers. The chair of the Committee was Mrs Coatman, who described the scheme as offering "homeliness" for lonely women. In 1944 they opened another club in Newton Heath in a former furniture store.

In November 1942 the YWCA opened a small reception hostel for women war-workers who had either been transferred to Manchester, but had arrived by train too late to get to their billets in the blackout, or were between trains, and needed somewhere to rest for a couple of hours. This was housed at 8 Greenwood Street, off Corporation Street, where the Ministry of Works and Planning had adapted the building to house 19 travellers. The resident warden was Mrs F A Heald, and the hostel offered a "cheery canteen" and lounge, as well as four bedrooms heated by electricity.[13]

Nurseries in War Time

Ernest Bevin, a former trade unionist, was aware that to get more married women into war work proper child care was essential, and that it would have to be greatly extended from the patchy provision available at the start of the war. However, nurseries were the province of the Ministry of Health which insisted that only qualified nurses should look after children. There was a tussle between the two Ministries, with the Ministry of Health often denying that there was a demand for nurseries. A memorandum at the Ministry of Labour outlined the problems they were facing:

Although in some areas, where the Medical Officer approves of day nurseries, the proposal has been made willingly, in the majority of areas the Medical Officer of Health greatly prefers that women with young children should remain at home and does not feel inclined to make much effort to persuade his Council to incur their share of the cost.[14]

The tardy approach of the Ministry of Health led to resolutions in favour of nurseries being passed at TUC Women's Conferences in 1941 and 1942, and also at the Labour Party Women's Conference. In some areas women set up campaigns and lobbied their local authority for nurseries. As the need for war workers grew ever more urgent the Ministry of Labour won the battle. Women were now sent to work in nurseries after a two week training course, and consequently the number of nurseries rose dramatically, with many of them based in huts.

Some firms around Manchester opened nurseries to encourage women to work

Young children in war-time nursery, 1940

there. In November 1942, for instance, Ashton Brothers, a cotton-spinning mill in Hyde, converted their recreation club - housed in two former army huts - into a nursery for under-fives, children of women who had recently started working at the mill. The nursery had capacity for up to 50 children, and unusually also took very young babies. The staff comprised a superintendent, Mrs Ogden, who was the mill's welfare officer, a registered nurse, two Child Care Reserve workers, and a pupil nurse. The nursery joined half a dozen other ones opened by firms in Lancashire and Cheshire, and 31 nurseries in Manchester and Salford run by public health authorities.[15]

The provision of nurseries was very much seen by the government as an emergency temporary measure, and it was assumed that once the war was over women would return home. In fact, in the spring of 1945, even before the war ended, nurseries were being closed at the rate of ten a month.

In April 1945 a Northern Nurseries Campaign Committee (NNCC), comprising some 50 organisations, was set up to put the case to the government for the retention of day nurseries. The NNCC collected evidence from mothers and matrons in Salford, the majority of whom thought that nurseries had improved the health, habits and happiness of the children. In addition to nursery schools, the campaigners wanted day nurseries to be retained as part of the essential health services of the country. At this point there were still 34 nurseries in Manchester and 15 in Salford.[16]

On 12 November Mrs Freda Grimble, organiser of the London Women's

Parliament, led a deputation to the Ministry of Health to press for a definite answer by the Labour government as to whether they were prepared to keep funding the full costs of nurseries as they had done during the war. According to Mrs Dunton from the NNCC, almost all the mothers they had contacted - who used nurseries in 30 local authority areas in Lancashire and Cheshire - thought that nurseries were necessary in peace-time.[17]

The NNCC was based at Gaddum House in Manchester. The Secretary was Frances Hancock, who in February 1946 wrote that the nurseries had carried out: **splendid work during war-time, releasing a large percentage of female labour, and at the same time increasing the health and happiness of the children. For the sake of the children alone it would surely be worthwhile to keep the nurseries open. The need for the retention of the day nurseries is vital in the industrial North, where there are so many mothers who must work in order to increase the family income. In addition, there are war widows, unmarried mothers, and mothers with disabled children, whose only alternative, if the nurseries close, is to go back to the system of "minders," a practice which cannot be too strongly condemned.**[18]

The NNCC campaign ran for several years after the end of the war. On 5 October 1946 they held a conference in Manchester at which Mrs Reed, matron of St Mary's hospital, told the delegates that they had to reorganise the whole of the nursery movement now that the war was over and gear it to the problems of the peace. The time had come, she continued, when nurseries should cease to be "mere appendages to industry" and become guardians of family life, helping to maintain a high standard of motherhood. Dr J D Kershaw, Medical Officer for Accrington, said that provision of nurseries was part of a social problem. "We have got to have women in industry in the North-west and we have got to make provision for the children of those women."[19]

In January 1949 the NNCC lobbied the Manchester Health Committee in protest on its policy on nurseries. At the meeting Councillor R E Thomas said that in 1947 Manchester had 29 nurseries with accommodation for 450 children, but applications had been received from 4,780 mothers, whilst many thousands of other women did not apply because they knew there was no reasonable chance of getting a place.[20]

In October 1952 the NNCC held another conference at Gaddum House, and the following month joined with other organisations in protesting against higher day charges introduced by Lancashire County Council and Manchester City Council, with some charges more than doubling. The Ministry of Health refused to meet a delegation from the campaign. I have not been able to find any further references to the campaign after 1952.

Exchange Visits of War Workers

Following the exchange visit of four male British war workers for four American ones in the autumn of 1943, a similar exchange visit of women war workers took place in 1945. The four British women were nominated by the TUC, and included Barbara Bates from Wythenshawe, an engineering worker and a member of the National Union of General and Municipal Workers.

Barbara was aged 42, and lived with her married sister at 50, Benchill Road, in Wythenshawe. She had worked in light engineering for 20 years, including a number of years at Metropolitan-Vickers and Parkinson and Cowan. She had been a shop steward for six years, had studied for a year at Hillcroft College for Working Women, and was currently women's recruitment officer for her union. Barbara said that she would be able to tell the American people, especially the women, of the great work British women had done in the war, particularly the older women and the married women "who have had two jobs to do and done them wonderfully well."

The four American women war workers spent six weeks in England, including a week in the North West in the first week in March. They were Grace E Woods Blackett, Julia O'Connor Parker, Maida Stewart Springer and Anna Murkovich. Mrs Springer, a member of the International Garments Workers' Union, was a black woman, the first to represent the American Federation of Labour abroad. They returned to the USA in April. The British women were still in the United States and a dinner in honour of the eight women was held in Washington. Miss Frances Perkins, Secretary of Labour, who attended told those present that "without the millions of women in all the Allied countries who acquired new skills and carried on their work steadily and faithfully we would not be so far along towards victory."

The Lancashire Women's Parliament

In 1941 and 1942 a number of Women's Parliaments were held in different parts of the country to discuss the issues thrown up by women going into war work. Although it was initiative stemming from the Communist Party, it drew in wider support than just their own membership, a sign that the changed position of women in society and the economy created by the war was leading to a thoughtful discussion of wider issues.

The first Women's Parliament took place in London on 13 July 1941 - just a few weeks after Nazi Germany had invaded the Soviet Union - and was attended by 346 women, who were dubbed "MPs." The Parliament was opened by Beatrix Lehmann, a well-known actress and author, who said: **We welcome you to this first session of the Women's Parliament, which meets at a time of crisis unparalleled in world history. We women, more than any, are sensible of the sufferings which have been brought upon this generation. We know what a terrible cost would be exacted by the victory of Fascist reaction and we know that the utter annihilation of Fascism must precede all hope of a just and lasting peace. Yet any who think that the role of a woman at this time is to sit down and weep beneath the load of her sufferings and take no part in the shaping of events, is mistaking all the lessons of history. The war, it is true, has broken up the settled course of social life. But it also faces us with new** responsibilities and immense opportunities.[21]

The printed report of the event said that the gathering was "confident of its strength and resolute in its purpose. They were not there to air grievances or bewail their fate, but to put forward concrete proposals." The Parliament passed an emergency resolution of support for the USSR, and at later sessions put forward draft Bills on Wages and Part-Time Work. These said that "to utilise the whole resources of the nation in the war against German Nazism and to ensure an early victory, it is necessary to bring about the most effective and fullest mobilisation of man power and woman power."

The Lancashire Women's Parliament took place on 12 April 1942, and was organised by Manchester and District Anglo-Soviet Women's Unity Committee. It was held in the Co-operative Hall, Downing Street, and attended by 300 women from political parties, trade unions, Anglo-Soviet committees, munition factories, and many other bodies. Also present were two representatives from the Ministry of Information, as well as a large number of other visitors. (This was the only meeting of the Lancashire Women's Parliament that I have been able to trace.)

Miss Clara Bamber, President of the Manchester and District Women's Anglo-Soviet Unity Committee, presided over the conference. She was active in the Co-operative Movement, and also Chair of the Manchester, Salford and District Maternal Mortality Committee.

In her opening address she said that about half the delegates represented women in industry, and about half represented housewives or organisations interested in women's work, thereby representing a very good cross section of Lancashire women. Clara explained that the Parliament had come about after a number of Manchester women had met the previous August and decided to form an Anglo-Russian Women's Friendship Committee. This had been very successful and a deputation had been sent to Madame Maisky (wife of the Soviet Ambassador) with donations of money and supplies to the Soviet Union.

Report of the Lancashire Women's Parliament

They had also affiliated to the Anglo-Russian Friendship Committee, started by the Lord Mayor of Manchester.

She recalled that when the Soviet trade union delegation had visited Manchester, Madame Nikolayeva, Secretary of the All-Union Council of Trade Unions, told them that she was disappointed at seeing so many women in Lancashire who were not working in industry. (The delegation had visited Manchester in January 1942, attending a conference, and also visiting bombed areas and factories.)

They had called the Parliament, continued Clara, to give women the opportunity of discussing why more of them were not working in industry and what the difficulties were which kept them out. In conclusion she spoke about the international situation:

At the moment the only country which is holding the enemy is Russia and Russia must be helped if we are to help ourselves. Their magnificent stand this winter has given us quiet nights; it has saved us from possible invasion and has filled us with admiration and courage. We love our land, too, and we will sacrifice for it, but we want the burden to fall equally on all people. Our deliberations today are to that end.[22]

Renold and Coventry Chain company, 1945

Women factory workers

The first item discussed by the delegates was the draft Women's Power Bill which set out the following demands in order to allow women to go into industry:
- Factory canteens and British restaurants
- Nursery schools and residential nurseries
- Full time education, dinners for all school children, breakfasts and teas for children of war-workers
- Play Centres for children of school age with voluntary supervision
- Full use of local part-time labour to made by all factory management
- All women who registered for National Service should be drawn into work without delay or class distinction
- An immediate examination of Lancashire industry should be undertaken by the Ministry of Labour, the employers and the trade unions with a view to making the fullest use of the available woman labour

Mrs Holt, representing the BRD Aircraft Factory in Warrington, moved the Bill. She said that she had wasted 12 years of her life as an unpaid housewife, but for the past five months she had been in industry helping the war effort. "The splendid and dauntless courage of the Soviet women drew me to the factory," she declared. "The Soviet women are an example to us, and we can play our part just as they are doing...every woman must play her part as more and more men are taken out of industry and drafted into the Forces." She went on to say that her factory was now 100 per cent trade union, and that as a senior shop steward she knew the problems confronting the women in industry such as the lack of nursery schools and shopping facilities. She asked the women of the Parliament to give this draft bill their utmost support.[23]

Bessie Wild, from the Longsight Anglo-Soviet Committee, said that there could be no future for her two children unless she herself played her part in the war effort. Her children attended a nursery and she was extremely satisfied with the manner in which her children were being looked after. Bessie had heard that a munitions factory quite near to her home was being opened, but when she presented herself she was told that there could be no question of part-time work. She thought that Labour Exchanges should adopt a more friendly and helpful attitude.[24]

Margaret Hyndman, described as a shop steward in "a large aircraft industry" (clearly the Avro factory in Chadderton which was making Lancaster bombers), said that the firm employed 11,000 workers, 2,000 of whom were women. They were not organised at first, but now they had a woman convenor as well as a male convenor. They had good conditions, and surprised the management by turning out the new bomber in three months under schedule. "The shop stewards," she continued, "took up the question of the canteen and secured substantial improvements, such as weekly dinners at six shillings per week, table-cloths, flowers on the tables, waitresses, good service, food well cooked and served. Since the women had started working at the factory, production had doubled. Get the women organised, and then we can end the war this year."[25]

Florence Mitton, a delegate from the Stretford branch of the TGWU at Metro-Vickers, said that she represented 2,000 members, and their worst problem was shopping which had led to much absenteeism. "We feel that in Manchester and Lancashire we should get busy on solving this problem – show the traders the difficulties experienced by the workers and get their co-operation in the settlement of the problem." She added that it was essential to get crèches.[26]

There was concern in the higher echelons of the trade union movement at the success of the Women's Parliaments, and the fact that it might enhance the standing of the Communist Party. Consequently Walter Citrine, General Secretary of the TUC, sent out a letter to the trade union movement which was read at the monthly meeting of the Manchester and Salford Trades Council on 17 January 1943.

It was clear, he wrote, that the Women's Parliaments were attempting to deal with many matters that were the subject of "negotiation by individual trade unions or the trade unions generally" and had intervened in matters that were essentially the responsibility of trade unions. If the Women's Parliaments were to receive support from trade union branches, district committee, or trades councils it would inevitably lead to "conflicting policies or misunderstandings." In all circumstances, the letter concluded, the General Council of the TUC strongly advised affiliated organisations and Trades Councils not to support the Women's Parliaments.

The letter was in some sense unnecessary, since the Women's Parliament in Lancashire was the last such meeting to be held. Henceforth the Communist Party directed its efforts towards factory production committees, and also a campaign for a Second Front, which called for an Allied invasion of Western Europe in order to assist the Red Army in its fight against the German armies in the East.

Ellen Wilkinson's War

Ellen was vehemently opposed to the Conservative Prime Minister Neville Chamberlain, adamant that the Labour Party should not enter a war coalition under his premiership. For once she found herself in tune with the rest of the Labour leadership. Chamberlain resigned after the German invasion of France and on 10 May 1940 Winston Churchill became Prime Minister with the support of most of the House of Commons. The Labour Party immediately agreed to serve in a Coalition government under him, and at Churchill's invitation the Labour Party leader Clement Attlee selected a number of Labour MPs for government posts, including Ellen.

Surprisingly Churchill, despite the great political distance between them, was very keen on Ellen, and she returned the compliment, stating after her interview for a job that she felt she "had been in the presence of a very great man and a very great leader." Initially Ellen was given a junior ministerial post in charge of hardship tribunals, but by October she was working as joint Parliamentary Private Secretary to fellow Labour MP Herbert Morrison, who had just been appointed Home Secretary.

Morrison gave Ellen responsibility for air-raid shelters and the homeless, a huge and urgent task as German bombing of British cities began in earnest in the autumn of 1940, killing tens of thousands, and destroying hundreds of thousands of houses and businesses. On her first evening in her new post she visited the East End, and thereafter, according to Ellen, she spent most of her time in air-raid shelters, talking to the public and taking notes on how to improve things. She refused to use the official government shelter in the disused underground station in Down Street. The reporter for the *Daily Express* was impressed by the new Minister:

Going round with Ellen Wilkinson there were two things I liked about her, things that gave me confidence in her approach to the problem – her energy and her natural touch with these people. She talked to the wardens and would always stop to talk to some man or woman and find their points of view.[27]

Ellen quickly realised that the Anderson air-raid shelters - supposed to be used by the public in their back gardens - were in fact almost useless, while there were not enough public air-raid shelters for the people who needed them. Typically she swung into action, supervising the manufacture of stronger shelters (which became known as Morrison shelters after the Home Secretary), and bearing down on local authorities to force them to provide better public air-raid shelters.

On 1 July 1940 Ellen made a broadcast on BBC radio on the meaning of Nazi rule. She began by telling the audience that she had heard "...a young woman say recently 'If we cannot buy new clothes we might as well live under Hitler'... But have you thought out what life under the Nazis means to women?" she asked her listeners. "It means the subjection of the lives of everybody not to the state... but to a war machine run by a set of gangsters who have seized power. They can only keep that power, and their hold over their own people, by war. Their only use for women is that they should provide more and yet more children to keep that war machine going."

History, Ellen continued, showed that the firmness of people's resistance depended upon women, and that it was no use women thinking they could keep their comforts. "If we are worrying about what is going to happen to the ornaments on the mantlepiece our nation will fail. If we are ready to throw our most cherished objects at the head of the enemy the point of successful resistance is reached." She ended her broadcast by urging women to get involved in the war effort.[28]

The heavy bombing of London by the Luftwaffe from September 1940 onwards led 200,000 East Enders to seek shelter in the Tube stations, something the authorities, including Ellen, initially opposed, ordering London Transport to stop them. It seems that they feared that the Eastenders might refuse to come up again, a revealing insight into how little faith the authorities had in the people they purported to represent. Eastenders simply ignored the order, however, and eventually forced the government to run the deep shelters properly and organise essentials such as sanitation and washing facilities.

Visiting the East End in October, Ellen promised people, "Safety, Sanitation, Sleep," and said that she intended to get a number of women using the shelters to call upon her and have a talk, adding that she did not think there was a general case for segregation of the sexes, but there was a case for the segregation of the old and sick, and also of young

An air raid shelter in a London Underground station in London during The Blitz.

women who had to rush from work to get a place in a shelter. "I do think that life should consist of something more than work and shelter."[29]

Ellen made good on her promise. A few weeks later she met a delegation of 26 women, both young and middle-aged, to talk about shelter problems over the inevitable cups of tea. Afterwards Ellen said,

"These women talked more sense about shelter conditions than I have heard from any of the expert committees that I have sat on up to date. We talked a good deal about the Tube. They said that one trouble was children got into the Tube, often as early as eight in the morning, and asked people for pennies, promising to keep places for them. There was general agreement among them that there should be a ticket system…They thought that wardens should be appointed by some central authority, and that they should be carefully chosen."[30]

Ellen made many visits to towns and cities up and down the country to see things for herself, and often returned to her home city of Manchester. On 3 December 1940 she visited Liverpool before travelling over to Manchester to tour the air-raid shelters at night, seeing half a dozen strutted basement shelters, as well as one built in the bed of an old canal.

She found that several required cleaning up, and also remarked on the general need for ventilation and heating. Ellen was taken to one basement shelter not on the official tour after a woman she'd met told her she ought to see it for herself. On viewing, Ellen judged it overcrowded, and the air "pretty foul," while those using it complained bitterly that they had no heat or ventilation, and that places were not individually allocated. Before she left Manchester Ellen demanded assurances from the hapless local officials accompanying her that things would be put right the very next day.

"You have got to realise that the provincial towns have only recently been given permission to do these things," she told the press when the tour was over. "It is a great advantage to me to visit the shelters myself. One sees the problem just as it is, and knows what to recommend to the Minister. I hope that when we have bunked and heated and lit the surface shelters we shall reverse the tendency to leave them empty and overcrowd the basements." She announced that the Ministry would now provide finance for the employment of paid shelter wardens in large provincial shelters, enabling shelters, such as the one in the crypt of a Salford church, to remain open day and night, instead of just during alerts.[31]

The Manchester Emergency committee was stung by Ellen's criticism of one shelter, which she had described as "just filthy," and issued a lengthy report the day after her visit. They maintained that it was cleaned every day, but children who were being sent there in the early evening used it as a playground, and were not using the toilet pails provided, but the corners of the shelter instead. "Many people who use the shelter are filthy in their habits, and every morning the shelter is strewn with all sorts of rubbish," they alleged.[32]

Ellen was a frequent radio broadcaster, both on the BBC and on the American networks. In January 1941 she broadcast to the USA about the experiences of women during the bombing. She recalled that one morning she had gone from the shelter to her office, where she found that all doors and windows were open. "'Fresh air is all very well,' I said, 'but isn't this rather excessive?' My secretary, a young Scottish girl, said calmly, 'They have just sent word that there is a huge bomb behind here that hasn't gone off yet. If it does, it will blow all the doors and windows out if they aren't open. Are you ready for your letters now?'" She also recalled being on Regent Street, and seeing two women who were looking in a shop window when the siren went off. "The women glanced up. 'There's Jerry,' said one, casually. 'Here's the sort of hat I want', said the other, and they went on looking at the window."

Ellen told listeners that her work often took her into the worst-bombed areas when the Blitz was on. "On occasions my officials and I have had to lie down flat while bombs burst near us. I have never seen any shrieking, hysterical women rushing about, though I have seen and talked to sobbing women whose houses have been bombed." She concluded her talk by looking to the future. "We are in acute danger. We know it. We face a worse three months than anything we have had yet. But, somehow, in that deep, unconscious mind of the tribe that one can feel functioning in times of crisis like this, we know that the tide has turned."[33]

In April 1941 Ellen came back to Manchester to study the shelters and confirmed that Morrison shelters were on their way to the city. In an interview she pointed out that the making of shelters had to be sandwiched into the full flow of war production, and that they had had to use smaller factories, some of which had been damaged by bombing, leading to a delay in some components arriving. The following month she returned again to speak at a parade of women's services in Longford Park, Stretford. Ellen said, "We cannot let Britain burn down. I shall still go on with my shelter work. A good deal of the organising of it is done, but air raid shelter work must change with the changing strategy of the enemy. Air-raid shelters are provided for able-bodied people to rest in, and sleep in if necessary, between their duties. They are not provided as a refuge from doing their duty to the country." She wanted to ensure that every woman who was called up to do fire-watching was given training, so that she knew exactly what to do. "I believe we are going to find that among those women who were considered on the shelf we shall find a great reserve of just sheer toughness when it comes to keeping fit to fight Hitler."[34]

Ellen returned to Manchester on 18 November 1941 to speak in the Albert Hall on Peter Street at a meeting to mark the 55th anniversary of the Manchester and Salford Methodist Mission. In her speech she looked back to her childhood, recalling that when she was a girl she used to go with her mother to the Central Hall midday service, racing off from school clutching a penny for the tram fare so that she could be back for her lessons by two o'clock. She told the audience that these services - which on a Sunday had seemed routine and ordinary - were much more exciting in those conditions, so perhaps her mother was wiser than she knew. Ellen maintained that religious activity created standards in public life and morality, remembering many Manchester meetings that were neither narrowly religious nor narrowly political eg protests against Congo atrocities, the Black and Tans in Ireland, repression in India or sweated labour at home.

She said that she believed that they had succeeded because they had a standard of public morality to appeal to, and that the real horror of the Nazi ruler was his refusal to refer any question to any standard except his own will for power. "There are those," she continued, "who, I am sure with the best possible intentions, are continually urging us to copy the methods of those we are fighting. Then it is we have to remember what we are fighting against is not the flesh and blood of Germans, who are individuals like ourselves, but the destruction of those standards, and that everything we are fighting for is lost and the sacrifices of our men are in vain if we lower those standards in the belief that that is realistic and that to keep standards in a war like this is mere sentimentality." Looking to the future, she concluded, she could say no more than that "good men and women should make peace."[35]

On 2 December 1942 Ellen again visited Manchester as part of a tour of regional cities to discuss arrangements for amending the regulations for fire-guards. At the press conference she said that she had been discussing a number of issues such as the target areas where women would not have to serve; the question of men who escaped fire-guard duty because there was no order where they lived; and people who regularly employed substitutes. Ellen added that she wished to remove the impression that women would not be asked to perform fire-guard duty so long as there were any men in their area who were not doing it. She described the fire-guard service as the most comprehensive piece of national service the country had ever been asked to do, and that some women volunteers who had been told that they would not be needed at their place of work were "highly indignant" because they would not share in the social arrangements made for fire-guards.[36]

Ellen suffered from ill-health on a number of occasions during the war, very likely because of her unrelenting work schedule. In July 1940 she was taken to hospital with appendicitis and had to be operated on. In August 1942 she banged her head when the car taking her home was in collision with a lorry, resulting in a slight fracture. In January 1943 Ellen and a number of other MPs were involved in a glider crash in which she sustained a double fracture of her ankle. In December 1944 her doctors stopped her presiding over the Labour Party conference because she was suffering from pneumonia and acute bronchitis.

The end of the war

On 30 April 1945 Adolf Hitler committed suicide in his besieged bunker in Berlin, after which German armies across Europe began surrendering. On 6 May the annual Manchester May Day procession took place from Albert Square to Platt Fields, organised by the Manchester and Salford Council of Labour, which was a mile long with many banners and flags and brass bands playing. The speakers in the park included Harold Laski, chairman of the Labour Party, and Dorothy Elliott, women's officer of the General and Municipal Workers Union. Laski said that the war had been won by the collective efforts of men and women everywhere and the time was long overdue to put ordinary men and women in power: to return a Tory government was to return the monopolists to power. The following day Germany surrendered unconditionally.

Victory in Europe was celebrated across the country on 8 May. In Manchester large crowds gathered in the city centre and stayed there until late in the evening. The *Manchester Guardian* reported:

The central thoroughfares were crowded even after darkness had set in, the younger people, and men and women of the services, being full of explosive high spirits. At ten o'clock Albert Square had become a great dancing floor, upon which partnerships were formed on a free and easy plan. Music came from the Town Hall and reached the crowd through loudspeakers.

A popular prank was to climb on to the roofs of the air raid shelters to dance – probably it was the men of the Navy who began it, but whoever set the example found abundant followers and presently the girls of the WAAF and the ATS showed a readiness to participate. Without ceremony dozens of them were hauled and pushed to the top amidst a good deal of cheering.

Fireworks were occasionally thrown into the air, and there was an unexpected supply of paper hats, streamers, confetti and other carnival accessories which, after years of a paper famine, would have been thought to be unobtainable.

Although the young people were sometimes very boisterous, the city police declared that "the crowd" in the central streets of the city was the least troublesome they had known. At the centres where Service men and women gathered, there was of course much jubilation. The workers at the NAAFI Club said it had been excessively crowded all day. The YMCA and the King George Services Club entertained almost innumerable guests, and the American Red Cross, where dancing continued well into the morning, was virtually a "free house" for soldiers' guests.

Little effort was made at floodlighting in the city. Apart from the Town Hall the chief contributions were those of the two largest stores in Market Street and a funfair in Oldham Street. The Transport Department's illuminated tramcar was the success of the evening and its progress through the city was accompanied by resounding cheers.

Piccadilly Gardens, which were crowded with people all the day and evening, suffered considerable damage, almost every blade of grass being trampled out of existence. Until a late hour, however,

Labour Party election programme 1945

Women celebrating VE Day in Manchester

Programme for Manchester May Day, 1945

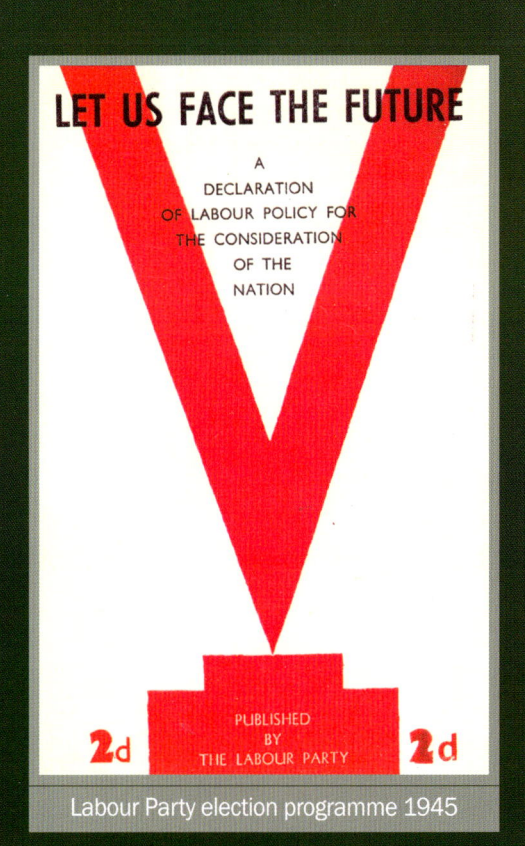

the most careful efforts were made to avoid harming the flowers and it was only as darkness began to fall that they suffered any serious damage.

Cross Street, outside the American Red Cross Club, was the scene late at night of a firework display, which appeared to be provided by American soldiers. Crimson flares were lighted in the middle of the road, and those nearest formed a ring and danced around them until the light died down. The performance was watched by a large crowd that blocked the road, and by a few patient motorists whose cars were held up on the edge of the crowd.[37]

Labour comes to power.

The Labour Party manifesto, published in April 1945, was called *Let Us Face the Future*, co-authored by Michael Young, Herbert Morrison, and Ellen Wilkinson. It reminded the public of the Depression years and declared that "the Labour party stands for freedom - for freedom of worship, freedom of speech, freedom of the Press...But there are certain so-called freedoms that Labour will not tolerate: freedom to exploit other people; freedom to pay poor wages and to push up prices for selfish profit; freedom to deprive the people of the means of living full, happy healthy lives." It pledged itself to full employment: "No more dole queues in order to let the Czars of Big Business remain kings in their own castles. The price of so-called 'economic freedom' for the few is too high and bought at the cost of idleness and misery for millions."

Labour proposed state action to ensure full employment, advocating the nationalisation of key industries, an urgent housing programme, the creation of a national health service, and a welfare state based on the 1942 Beveridge Report, which had set out proposals to end "the five Giant Evils": Want, Disease, Ignorance, Squalor and Idleness.

The Report advocated a contribution-based social insurance scheme which would provide universal benefits for unemployment, sickness or old age in times of need, although National Assistance (as it was to be called), would be set a low level to discourage "malingerers." Beveridge's view of women remained traditional: he assumed that at the end of the war married women would return home and wrote that their prime task was "to ensure the continuation of the British race" which "at its present rate of reproduction...cannot continue."

On 21 May Ellen Wilkinson presided over the 44th Labour Party conference in Blackpool, the largest ever held in the party's history. In her opening speech she spoke of how people must decide "whether Britain will put itself under the rule of Big Business, or whether we will advance towards a society in which the whole resources of the country are efficiently used in the interest of the community." She told the audience that the Labour party wanted millions of houses, jobs for all, social security, educational opportunity for everyone and a health service. In her final speech Ellen said that they were fighting "the Party of the rich, the Party of the powerful, the Party of big business, the party that controls the great industries, the cartels and very largely the press. These are our enemies." "This is the proudest moment of my life," she concluded.

The election was held on 5 July, although the counting did not finish until 26 July to allow for the votes of men and women serving abroad in the armed services to arrive and be included. The Tories, imagining that Churchill would reap the rewards of being a very popular war leader, were confident that they would win, as had happened in December 1918 in the wake of victory in the First World War.

But it was the Labour Party who were triumphant. They won 393 seats (47% of the vote) while the Tories won 197 seats (36%) and the Liberals won 12 seats (9% of the vote). The Communist Party increased their representation to two MPs, with Phil Piratin joining Willie Gallacher in the Commons. Twenty-one women Labour MPs were elected, the highest ever number.

Labour were victorious because, having endured six years of conflict, millions wanted a better kind of society than that which had existed before the war. The Labour manifesto chimed with the popular mood.

The party also benefited from having been part of the war-time coalition government in which ministers such as Ernest Bevin, Herbert Morrison and Ellen Wilkinson had proved what they could do in office. During the war the state had taken on so many functions that it no longer seemed such a leap of faith to imagine using its power to achieve a better, more equal society.

Over the next five years the Labour government implemented the biggest social changes in fifty years, creating the National Health Service and a new Social Security system, as well nationalising the mines, the steel industry and the railways.

These profound social changes were popular, and when the Tory government returned to power in 1951, it left most of them in place. It was not until 1979 with the election of a Tory government, led by Margaret Thatcher - who was ideologically committed to ending the post-war consensus - that these measures were overturned, and a new era of political and social division began. But that is another story.

Notes

[1] *Manchester Guardian*, 2 September 1939, p. 10.

[2] www.bbc.co.uk/history/ww2peopleswar/stories/93/a2671193.shtml

[3] *Manchester Guardian*, 4 September 1939, p. 4.

[4] *Manchester Guardian*, 6 September 1939, p. 9.

[5] *Manchester Guardian*, 27 November 1939, p. 8.

[6] *Manchester Guardian*, 27 November 1939, p. 8.

[7] *Manchester Guardian*, 18 August 1944, p. 3.

[8] Penny Summerfield, *Women Workers in the Second World War*, (1984), p. 51.

[9] Edith Summerskill, "Women and Conscription" in Jenny Hartley (editor), *Hearts Undefeated; Women's Writing of the Second World War* (1994), pp. 108-109.

[10] *Manchester Guardian*, 25 June 1942, p. 4.

[11] Penny Summerfield, *Women Workers in the Second World War*, (1984), p. 146.

[12] *Manchester Guardian*, 23 October 1942, p. 7.

[13] *Manchester Guardian*, 6 November 1942, p. 6.

[14] Penny Summerfield, *Women Workers in the Second World War*, (1984), p. 78.

[15] *Manchester Guardian*, 14 November 1942, p. 6.

[16] *Manchester Guardian*, 25 August 1945, p. 3.

[17] *Manchester Guardian*, 13 November 1945, p. 3.

[18] *Manchester Guardian*, 27 February 1946, p. 4.

[19] *Manchester Guardian*, 7 October 1946, p. 6.

[20] *Manchester Guardian*, 29 January 1949. p. 6.

[21] *Report of First Session, London Women's Parliament* (1941), p. 3. One of Beatrix's last appearances on television was as Professor Rumford in the *Doctor Who* serial "The Stones of Blood," broadcast in the autumn of 1978. She died in July 1979.

[22] *Report on Lancashire Women's Parliament*, (1942), p. 2.

[23] *Report on Lancashire Women's Parliament*, (1942), p. 6.

[24] *Report on Lancashire Women's Parliament*, (1942), p. 10.

[25] *Report on Lancashire Women's Parliament*, (1942), p. 10.

[26] *Report on Lancashire Women's Parliament*, (1942), p. 16.

[27] Paula Bartley, *Ellen Wilkinson, from Red Suffragist to Government Minister* (2014), p. 104.

[28] *Manchester Guardian*, 2 July 1940, p. 2.

[29] *Manchester Guardian*, 11 October 1940, p. 5.

[30] *Manchester Guardian*, 22 October 1940, p. 6.

[31] *Manchester Guardian*, 4 December 1940, p. 5.

[32] *Manchester Guardian*, 6 December 1940, p. 6.

[33] *Manchester Guardian*, 13 January 1941, p. 8.

[34] *Manchester Guardian*, 28 April 1941, p. 2. *Manchester Guardian*, 15 May 1941, p. 6.

[35] *Manchester Guardian*, 19 November 1941, p. 2.

[36] *Manchester Guardian*, 3 December 1942, p. 2.

[37] *Manchester Guardian*, 9 May 1945, p. 8.

Afterword: Ellen Wilkinson's Peace 1945-1947

On 26 July 1945 Clement Attlee became Prime Minister, the first time a Labour Prime Minister had enjoyed a majority in the House of Commons since the party's foundation in 1900. There was just one woman in the Labour Cabinet, Ellen Wilkinson, whom Attlee made Minister of Education.

Paula Bartley, in her biography of Ellen, *Ellen Wilkinson: from Red Suffragist to Government Minister,* suggests that Attlee gave her a job (despite her preference for Herbert Morrison as leader) because she was popular, both with the party and with the public. In addition there is always an advantage in penning your critics within the Cabinet, thereby preventing them from publicly expressing dissent.

In September 1945 Ellen spoke at the National Conference of Labour Women in Leeds, beginning by stating that "the most mischevious thing that can be said abroad to-day is that Britain is a second class power just because our overseas assets have gone." She posed a question to her audience: "What makes a first-class power?" Ellen then attempted an answer, observing that history was full of instances of nations with great material wealth sinking rapidly into obscurity, because they did not know how to use their assets, and squandered them in the luxury of the few and neglect of the people. She continued:

The British people have shown they are willing to try out new ideas, willing to work for planned country. It is the job of the Ministry of Education to use the Great Education Act as a storehouse of mental machine tools to sharpen for Britain the brains that are to meet the new situation. On the technical side we are expanding rapidly both in the new junior technical colleges and in preparations that are being made for high-grade adult training and post-graduate research...the Ministry of Education is already training the designers for new industries and bringing back older ones we have lost. We are planning to pay special attention to scientific development.[1]

Her priorities as Minister were to implement the 1944 Education Act; to raise the school leaving age to 15; and to expand and improve technical education in order to rebuild the country's post-war economy.

Attlee asked Ellen to go to defeated Germany to visit the schools and assess the situation. Just months after the end of the war, this was a country of burnt and bombed out cities and countless widows, millions of men having died in Hitler's war. On 3 October she visited Hamburg where she saw children eating a mid-day meal of vegetable soup in cellars formerly used as air-raid shelters. Next day she visited schools in Berlin, including going to some schools in the Soviet zone. The children here looked pale and undernourished, and were wearing their costs in the classroom because the windows had no glass. When Ellen asked the children what they had had for breakfast, most of them told her that they had just had bread or coffee without milk. By contrast in the British Zone in Berlin, as in Hamburg, the children were being given vegetable soup at mid-day.

During her visit Ellen met Military Government education officers and German educationists, whom she told to "let children think for themselves." She also spoke to pupils and teachers, discovering that many schools were operating a shift system with one group of pupils being taught in the morning and another in the afternoon. On a visit to a boys' secondary school Ellen was surprised at how good their English was and made a speech to them.

She told the press that many of the teachers she had met had spent years in concentration camps and were now doing their best to rebuild the education system, although many schools had been destroyed, while there was a shortage of books and teachers.

On her return to England Ellen said that the devastation she had seen was "something beyond comprehension" and that:

Children are very backward, and whether their education can continue during the winter depends on the production and distribution of coal. At some schools I visited the children were taken into the school yards because, although the day was cold, it was warmer there in the sunshine than in the draughty buildings. I did not find so much severe malnutrition as I had expected. Where it is severe school meals are given, but not so many get the meals as we should like... There is no doubt that quite a number of children will die before the winter ends as food cannot be got to them. That was principally in Berlin, which is the central problem. There is a scheme to evacuate some of the children into country areas.[2]

Ellen wrote a secret memorandum in which she recorded her impressions. In the British Zone there were more than two million displaced people and more than two million German troops living in the open, while thousands of refugees from the Soviet Zone were entering every

page 57

day. The Allied bombing and invasion had destroyed the administration and much of the transport and power systems. There were shortages of food, coal and housing, while serious diseases such as diphtheria and tuberculosis were a threat. Life was dangerous with many murders and rapes. She said that in the Soviet Zone the Russians were "not worrying very much about what happens to the Germans and in particular how many of them die or contract diseases during this winter...Russians are stripping the zone which they occupy of as much material and plant as they can carry away to Russia."[3]

Ellen inherited the 1944 Education Act, put through the Commons by the Tory "Rab" Butler, which set out a "tripartite" selective system with grammar schools for those children deemed to be intellectually gifted; secondary moderns for the majority of pupils ; and technical schools for young people interested in science or engineering. Pupils were to be selected at the age of eleven by taking an exam. Those who passed the exam went to the grammar school, those who failed (and the word "failed" was used) went to the secondary modern.

How much Ellen really believed in the Education Act is open to question. The left-wing journal *Tribune* commented, "We do not doubt that she will strive to instil into it the maximum socialist content, but it is not the act which she would have fashioned if she could have started afresh." Ellen seems to have believed that the three types of schools would have parity of esteem, but in reality middle-class parents moved heaven and earth to get their children through the 11-plus and into grammar schools which catered for approximately 20% of pupils.

Characteristically, having taken on a job, she put her heart and soul into it, badgering her Cabinet colleagues for money to build new schools and train the teachers she needed. Her fellow MP Susan Lawrence reflected, "...I never doubted that in spite of all the frightful obstacles - want of teachers and want of buildings - that Ellen would find a way, and she did where a weaker minister might well have shrunk from all the lions in the park."

Ellen told the Labour party conference in 1946 that she had two guiding aims: **"...and they come largely out of my own experience. I was born into a working-class home, and I had to fight my own way through to the University. The first of those guiding principles was to see that no boy or girl is debarred by lack of means from taking a course of education for which he or she is qualified...the second one was that we should remove from education those class distinctions which are the negation of democracy."**[4]

Ellen did put forward a number of proposals that were supported by both left and right within the party, such as raising the school-leaving age from 14 to 15; providing free school milk to school children; reducing the number of direct grant schools; and introducing university scholarships for those who could not afford to go.

To raise the school-leaving age Ellen had to find money to pay 13,000 extra teachers and provide 5,000 more classrooms to cope with nearly 400,000 more children. After battles in Cabinet with her colleagues she succeeded, although she had to threaten to campaign outside Parliament at one point. With a pressing need for more teachers Ellen set up a one-year Emergency Training Scheme for ex-service women and men aged 25 to 30 who were given grants to enable them to undertake the course. The training was often carried out in temporary colleges around the country.

And with little money to build new schools, Ellen was forced to use pre-fabricated classrooms instead. She defended their use at the Labour Party conference. "I know that some of these huts look very functional ...but they generally are much cleaner, more sanitary and more weatherproof than many of the picturesque old buildings... They are not disused Army huts, they are proper huts, well designed for their job."[5]

On 1 March 1946 she returned to Manchester, having lunch at the Town

Ellen Wilkinson in her school photograph (third from left, back row)

German children in Berlin being fed at school

Grave of Ellen Wilkinson in Penn Street churchyard

Ellen Wilkinson in Manchester, 1946

Hall, and then visiting Palmerston Street primary school. After this she paid a visit to her old school, Ardwick Central, where students from the Manchester School of Art (many of them former pupils) formed a guard of honour when she arrived. The school pupils sang three songs of welcome and she was given a framed photograph of "Miss Swithenbank's Class March 1905," showing a "long-haired alert looking young girl named Ellen Wilkinson."

She told the audience that she had once been told off for singing out of tune, and had never dared sing since! She also recalled that in her day "headmasters were headmasters," and that as a punishment she had once been taken out of Standard V Girls and put in Standard V Boys. Ellen then went on to the College of Domestic Economy where she opened an exhibition on "The Child and the Community." Miss Weddell, the college's principal, said that the exhibition was designed to illustrate the basic needs of children – good nutrition, good physical conditions, and a fine stimulating environment.

Ellen made a short speech, stating that the exhibition underlined a valuable lesson, that no matter how excellent the teacher and how excellent the school, unless there was a minimum of security, of cleanliness and of nutrition at home, then the teacher's work would be frustrated, "I think we are learning that lesson as a nation and as a Government. You are starting your careers at a really exciting moment and at a moment when some of the frustrations that have made martyrdom of the lives of many people are being removed."[6]

Later that month Ellen was back in the north again, this time in Salford to give the address at Speech Day at Pendleton High School for Girls. In her speech she warned the girls that the time was coming when they, as the future mothers and teachers of the nation, would have to make a stand against what she called the "vulgarity and bad taste" now permeating public entertainment. She continued:

"We are now in an age of mass entertainment and unfortunately the people who are making great fortunes out of these things think they can do it by appealing rather to the lower side of human nature, to the people with no taste. There is a great flaming poster on Piccadilly Circus, on the walls of the biggest cinema in London, and the title of the film it is advertising is 'Getting Gerties's Garter'... It is things like that which you girls will have, as the arbiters of taste, to end."[7]

In the autumn of 1946 Ellen's health - never robust - began to worsen. In October she became ill whilst visiting Prague to attend a British Film Festival. The report in the *Manchester Guardian* said that she appeared to be on the point of collapse when she spoke briefly at the opening and had to cling to the microphone to remain standing. Ellen had to return to England, instead of going on to Paris as had originally been planned.

One of her last public engagements was on 24 January 1947 when Ellen opened the Old Vic Theatre School in the company of Laurence Olivier and others. She said that her aim was to make England a "Third Programme" nation, by which she meant that she would like to have a nation that knew so much about the standards of good music, of great drama and of the visual arts that those things became passionately needed necessities. Her Ministry was anxious to give all the practical help possible to students of the drama, because the value of drama in education – not only to children, but in the theatre -was realised. She finished by saying, "We should have our Old Vic open again to cheer us up."[8]

After being found in a coma Ellen was taken into hospital where she died on 6 February 1947 to the shock of her friends and colleagues. The inquest heard medical evidence that Ellen had had a heart attack after taking too many drugs prescribed for asthma and insomnia.

In the House of Commons Clement Attlee paid tribute to Ellen:

She had great courage and a burning sympathy for all those who suffered, which extended far beyond the bound of this country. She had visited many countries. I recall today how she marched from the North with the unemployed of Jarrow and her valiant efforts to bring assistance to that sorely stricken area. I recall visiting, in her company, Spanish Republicans during the course of the civil war. I remember her complete disregard for danger, and how, on a return journey, although her plane was struck by lightning, she got to this House in time to move her Bill on hire purchase which subsequently became law.

…The difficulties of bringing into force the Education Act in the conditions obtaining after the war, were very formidable, but she set herself to overcome them. It is sad that she could not have lived to see in operation the raising of the school age, for which she had striven so hard. She had great gifts of eloquence and had a trenchant and effective pen. She earned the respect and affection of all her comrades. To all of us who knew her well and worked with her, her memory will remain as that of a good comrade, a proud and brave spirit. I am sure that the sympathy of the House will go out to her sister, who was her companion for so many years.[9]

He was followed by Winston Churchill:

I rise to associate myself with the tribute which the Prime Minister has paid to the late Minister of Education. Miss Ellen Wilkinson served for five years and three months in the Administration of which I had the honour to be the head, and I can testify, from a different point of view, to the earnestness, zeal and sympathy with which she discharged all her work.

The Prime Minister has spoken about Jarrow and the grim winter of 1940–41. Constantly under the fire of the enemy, she was always pursuing her task and her duty, and giving the greatest possible aid to the measures which it was necessary to take in those days of great stress. Active, courageous, competent, accessible, she had many of the traits at which Ministers of every Government and of every party have been taught to aim. She had a very warm sympathy for social causes of all kinds, and was fearless and vital in giving expression to them. But she also had a great pride in our country and in its flag. This was very noticeable in several of her speeches and actions, not only during the crisis of the war, but later. She always wished to see this Island great and famous, and capable of offering a decent home to all its people.[10]

The *Manchester Guardian* remembered Ellen in its columns:

The death of Ellen Wilkinson will be felt nowhere more than in Manchester. Here she was born and bred, and although the city has seen little of her in later years she carried a tang of Manchester with her wherever she went. She brought to public affairs an acute mind, an ebullient spirit, and - the dominant thing in her – a passion for social justice, an intuitive and devoted partisanship for the poor and the weak which found a fertile field in the dismal years of deflation and unemployment between the wars. It was by a finely dramatic stroke of history that she became at last the member for Jarrow, most tragical and hopelessly smitten of all the victims of the great slump. She had a vein of intransigence; she could be an uncomfortable colleague as well as a ruthless opponent. She could write with force, wit and pith: letters or journalism lost a craftswoman to politics. But it is hard to think of her making a career in anything but the Labour movement... .She was the second woman to sit in the Cabinet…but probably she enjoyed the Ministry of Education less than her wartime position at the Ministry of Home Security where she could weave together the strands of policy and the warm direct contacts of the air-raid shelter, the warden's post, the rest centre for bombed-out families. Her last years have been given to the drive to train teachers and build classrooms enough to make possible the raising of the school leaving age without postponement; though she will not see it, she lived long enough to ensure that it should be so and to know that it would be so. Meredith bade us "plod on and keep the passion fresh." Plodding was not much in Ellen Wilkinson's line, but all politics are a plod and few politicians have ever kept the passion fresher.[11]

Ellen was buried in Penn Street near Amersham, where she shared a house with her sister, Annie. Her headstone reads simply "Ellen Wilkinson 1891-1947." When Annie died in 1963 she was buried in the same grave.

Notes

[1] *Manchester Guardian*, 6 September 1945, p. 3.

[2] *Manchester Guardian*, 8 October 1945, p. 5.

[3] Paula Bartley, *Ellen Wilkinson from Red Suffragist to Government Minister* (2014), p.128

[4] Bartley, pp.124-125.

[5] Bartley, p. 126.

[6] *Manchester Guardian*, 2 March 1946, p. 6.

[7] *Manchester Guardian*, 28 March 1946, p. 3. The film she was referred was a 1945 American slapstick comedy film written and directed by Allan Dwan, and starring Dennis O'Keefe, Marie McDonald, and Barry Sullivan. It hardly seemed to presage the fall of Western civilisation, as Ellen implied.

[8] *Manchester Guardian*, 25 January 1947, p. 5.

[9] *Hansard*, 6 February 1947.

[10] *Hansard*, 6 February 1947.

[11] *Manchester Guardian,* 9 Feb 1947, p. 4

About the Mary Quaile Club

The Mary Quaile Club was set up in December 2013 with the aim of holding regular discussions on working class history and the links with contemporary political issues facing working people today.

We take our name from Mary Quaile (1886 to 1958), an Irish migrant to Manchester. She rose from a café waitress to one of the most well-known women trade unionists in Britain. Mary was an organiser for the Manchester and Salford Women's Trades Council and later national women's officer for TGWU. She also served on the TUC General Council, and led a TUC women's trade union women's delegation to the Soviet Union for four months in 1925.

Since our foundation we have held many varied events which are listed below. We have also published two publications: *Northern ReSisters: conversations with radical women* and *Dare to Be Free: women in trade unions, past and present*; commissioned a play about Mary Quaile, *Dare to Be Free*; and set up a website on which we placed the complete minutes of the Manchester and Salford Trades Council, transcribed from the hand-written original volumes by Bernadette Hyland.

Full details of our activities can be found at https://maryquaileclub.wordpress.com.

Whatever Happened to the Welfare State?
15 February 2014. Cornerstone Cafe, Salford.
A discussion on the political career of Ellen Wilkinson and the crisis facing the NHS. Guest speakers: Paula Bartley (author of a biography of Ellen Wilkinson) and Hugh Caffrey (Keep Our NHS Public).

Revealing Truths: Just How Free is the Press?
29 April 2014. Friends Meeting House, Manchester.
Guest speakers: Granville Williams (Campaign for Press and Broadcasting Freedom) and Steve Kingston (*Salford Star*).

A Writer Looks at History
24 May 2014. Three Minute Theatre, Manchester.
We welcomed John Fay, writer of television dramas such as *Brookside, Coronation Street, Blue Murder and The Mill*. In a wide ranging, thoughtful, and never less than entertaining discussion John discussed how he became a writer, reflected on the various series he has written for… and a great deal more…

Screening of *Play for Today* "The Spongers" by Jim Allen (1978)
21 June 2014. Working Class Movement Library, Salford.
We were delighted that Jimmy McGovern joined us for the screening and the discussion.

Screening of Play for Today *United Kingdom*, by Jim Allen (1981)
27 September 2014. Three Minute Theatre, Manchester.
Guest speakers: Honor Donnelly (Anti-Bedroom Tax) and Andy Willis (University of Salford).

Hannah Mitchell Day
18 October 2014. Topaz Cafe, Ashton-under-Lyne.
A celebration of the life and politics of socialist and suffragette Hannah Mitchell (1871-1956) who lived in Ashton between 1900 and 1910. Guest speakers: Michael Herbert (Mary Quaile Club), Ciara O'Sullivan (Mary Quaile Club), Christine Clayton (environmental activist), Eileen Murphy (playwright) and Charlotte Hughes (anti-austerity campaigner).

Actress Rachel Austin read some short stories written by Hannah: balladress Jennifer Reid sang a number of songs.

Mary Quaile Day: A celebration of International Women's Day
21 March 2015 Methodist Central Hall, Manchester.
Guest speakers: Ciara O'Sullivan (Mary Quaile Club), Alison Ronan (historian), Hannah Ravenscroft (Unite), Susan Lyons (Women for Independence, Scotland), Laura and Ellen (Podemos) and Selma James (Wages for Homework).

We launched our first publication, *Northern ReSisters: Conversations with Radical Women* by Bernadette Hyland
6 June 2015. Working Class Movement Library, Salford.
Bernadette spoke about her reasons for writing the book: to record the experiences of northern women active in campaigns over the past 40 years and to offer their stories as an inspiration for new generations of activists. She was followed by Betty Tebbs, Linda Clair, Honor Donnelly, Mandy Vere and Christine Clark who are featured in the

book and who spoke about their personal experiences as activists.

The Headscarf Revolutionaries
3 October 2015. Working Class Movement Library, Salford.

Brian Lavery discussed his book *The Headscarf Revolutionaries* which looked back to 1968 at the remarkable and successful campaign waged by working class women in Hull, led by Lillian Bilocca, to get proper health and safety on trawlers after the loss of three trawlers in a matter of weeks. Hilda Palmer from the Greater Manchester Hazards Centre reflected on the struggle for proper health and safety at work and how the gains of the last 40 years were under assault as never before

Screening of *Play for Today* "The Lump" by Jim Allen (1967)
14 November 2015. Three Minute Theatre, Manchester.

This classic television play about building workers was produced by Tony Garnett. We were delighted that Tony was able to come up from London to be with us for this event.

Migrant Workers: Past and Present
9 April 2016. Working Class Movement Library, Salford.

Chris Unsworth, author of The *British Herring Industry 1900-1960*, spoke about the forgotten story of Scottish women who migrated to England to work in the herring industry. Sandra Penaloza-Rice, co-ordinator and co-founder of Migrant Support Manchester, spoke about the position of migrant workers today, and how MSM is working to support them with education, cultural and other projects.

Premiere of our play *Dare to Be Free* by Jane McNulty
30 April 2016. Part of the Manchester May Day Festival. Manchester Mechanics Institute.

Dare To Be Free is set in the past and present. It's 1908 and waitresses in a Manchester cafe are fed up and ready to strike for proper pay and decent working conditions. It's 2016 and workers in a Manchester "fast food experience" are fed up and ready to strike for proper pay and decent working conditions. Linking the two eras is Mary Quaile, a pioneer of women's trade unionism in the C20th, come to help out her modern-day sisters because the issues she fought on 100 years ago are back with avengeance...

Dare to Be Free was also performed at the Inspire Centre, Levenshulme on 14 May, Bolton Socialist Club on 14 May, Glossop Labour Club on 15 May and Three Minute Theatre on 4 June.

"Dare to Be Free": women in trade unions, past and present
4 June 2016.

We launched our second publication, *"Dare to Be Free": women in trade unions, past and present* at Three Minute Theatre, Manchester, as part of the Manchester History Festival.

This publication has two parts: a biography of Mary Quaile written by Michael Herbert, followed by ten interviews with women of today active in trade unions at grass roots level, written by Bernadette Hyland. After Bernadette spoke we were delighted to welcome Sarah Woolley from the Baker's Union, and Khadija, Robert and Ana from the Hotel Workers branch of Unite in London.

We finished with the final performance of our play *Dare to Be Free*.

A complete screening of the television drama series *The House That Jack Built* by Shelagh Delaney
26 November 2016. Three Minute Theatre, Manchester.

Originally aired by the BBC in 1977, this was a rare screening of this series. Our thanks to the BFI and Home for their assistance in arranging this.

The Grunwick Strike 1976-1978
3 December 2016. Working Class Movement Library, Salford.

We looked back at the Grunwick Strike of 1976-1978, one of the most important industrial disputes of the 1970s when a group of mainly Asian women struck for union recognition at the Grunwick film processing plant in Willesden in the hot summer of 1976.

This event began with a screening of The Great Grunwick Strike, a film made by Chris Thomas in 2007 for Brent Trades Council.

page 63

Sujata Aurora from the Grunwick 40 Committee spoke about the importance of the dispute. She was followed by Lisa Turnbull from the Durham Teaching Assistants who spoke about their campaign against drastic wage reductions. Ian Allinson from UNITE at Fijutsu in Manchester spoke from the audience about their dispute.

Screening of the film *Business As Usual*

8 April 2017. Three Minute Theatre, Salford.
This film is based on a real story that took place in Liverpool in 1983 when shop manager Audrey White was sacked after objecting to the area manager's sexual harassment of young female staff. She won her job with the support of her union, TGWU, after the shop was picketed every day for five weeks.

We were delighted that Audrey could join us for the screening and speak about the story behind the film. Our second speaker was Sophie Shaw, Equalities representative of London Unite Hotel Workers Branch. She spoke about how sexual harassment is rampant in an industry where women are dependent on getting enough hours to make up their wages, and also the vulnerability of the many foreign workers.

Minutes of the Manchester and Salford Women's Trades Council

29 April 2017. Mechanics Institute, Manchester.
We launched the website of the complete minutes of the Manchester and Salford Women's Trades Council, 1895 – 1919. This was part of the Manchester May Day Festival.

This event was the culmination of a year-long project to transcribe the Minutes of the Council and place them on a website for all to read and make use of.

We were given the two volumes of hand-written Minutes by Mary Quaile's descendants in 2016 who made contact with us in the course of our research for our pamphlet *Dare to Be Free*.

At the launch Bernadette Hyland spoke about her work on the Minutes and the insights it had given her into the methods the organisers used to unionise women. She drew parallels with the current situation of low pay and zero hours contracts for many workers. Lisa Turnbull from the Durham Teaching Assistants spoke about their fight against a 23% pay cut threatened by their employers, Labour-controlled Durham County Council, a fight which had been built up by grassroots activism. Lisa then officially launched the website.
www.mswtuc.co.uk

Fighting Unemployment, Poverty and Austerity

30 September 2017. Working Class Movement Library, Salford.
Our first speaker was Sean Mitchell, author of *Struggle or Starve, Working Class Unity in Belfast in 1932*. He brought to life the story of how Protestants and Catholics united to demand equality and justice in the Poor Law system.

Our second speaker, Charlotte Hughes from Tameside against the Cuts, told the audience how the social security system was going backwards in its treatment of poor people. She spoke about some of the individual cases she had encountered and how her group worked to support individuals as well as publicising their activities through her blog, *The Poor Side of Life*.

"The World Is My Country": A Celebration of the Life and Writings of Thomas Paine

27 January 2018. Working Class Movement Library, Salford.
We revived the custom of celebrating the birthday of Thomas Paine. Guest speakers: Michael Herbert (Mary Quaile Club), Mandy Vere (News from Nowhere Bookshop) and Trevor Griffiths (writer of *These are the Times*).

Presentation of the Minutes of the Manchester and Salford Women's Trades Council to the Working Class Movement Library

10 March 2018.
We formally presented two volumes of the Minutes following the completion of our transcription project. Speakers: Bernadette Hyland (project researcher) and Maggie Cohen (Chair - WCML Trust). Actress Joan McGee read extracts from the Minutes.

Launch of the play collection, *Workers' Playtime*

19 May 2018. Three Minute Theatre, Manchester.
An evening of speeches, drama and song to launch a book of radical plays *Worker's Play Time*, edited by Doug Nicholls, General Secretary of the GFTU. We were very pleased that Doug could join us. In his address he outlined how cultural and artistic expression has always been integral to labour movement struggles.

Dreams and Nightmares: Feminist Utopias and Dystopias

6 October 2018. Levenshulme Old Library, Manchester.
Una McCormack discussed the work of Katherine Burdekin, whose work included the dystopian novel *Swastika Night* (1937). Ciara O'Sullivan discussed two utopian feminist novels: *Herland* (1915) by Charlotte Perkins Gilman and *Woman on the Edge of the Time* by Marge Piercy (1976).

Northern Radicalism in 1907: founding of the Gaiety Theatre, Manchester and founding of the National Union of Journalists

10 November 2018. Three Minute Theatre, Manchester. A joint event with the National Union of Journalists.
John Harding, author of *Staging Life: The Story of the Manchester Playwrights*, spoke about the founding of the Gaiety Theatre in Manchester by Annie Horniman. One of the Manchester playwrights was Harry Richardson. Tim Gopsill, (NUJ), author of *Journalists: a history of the NUJ*, spoke about the role of Harry in founding the NUJ and the challenges facing the union in the modern age.